NINA PARISH is a Sen

University of Bath, UK. Her research interests

and twenty-first-century French literature and the visual arts and in particular modernism, the avant-gardes, modern and contemporary poetry (including digital practice) and the artist's book. She has published a monograph, *Henri Michaux: Experimentation with Signs* (Amsterdam: Rodopi, 2007), and various articles on these subjects.

EMMA WAGSTAFF is a Senior Lecturer in French Studies at the University of Birmingham, UK, where she specialises in modern and contemporary French poetry and the connections between literature and the visual arts in the modern period. She has published various articles on those subjects, as well as *Provisionality and the Poem: Transition in the Work of Du Bouchet, Jaccottet and Noël* (Amsterdam: Rodopi, 2006) and *Writing Art: French Literary Responses to the Work of Alberto Giacometti* (Oxford: Peter Lang, 2011).

With Hugues Azérad and Michael G. Kelly, Nina Parish and Emma Wagstaff co-edited *Poetic Practice and the Practice of Poetics in French since 1945* (=spec. iss. of French Forum, 37, 1-2 (2012)), and *Chantiers du poèmes : Prémisses et pratiques de la création poétique contemporaine* (Oxford: Peter Lang, 2012). From 2012 to 2015, Nina Parish and Emma Wagstaff organised an international research network, funded by the Arts and Humanities Research Council, on interdisciplinary connections in contemporary French poetic practice (https://frenchpoetryand.wordpress.com/).

WRITING THE REAL

A BILINGUAL ANTHOLOGY OF CONTEMPORARY FRENCH POETRY

Edited by
Nina Parish and Emma Wagstaff

ENITHARMON PRESS

First published in 2016
by Enitharmon Press
10 Bury Place
London WC1A 2JL

www.enitharmon.co.uk

Distributed in the UK by
Central Books
50 Freshwater Road
Chadwell Heath
London RM8 1RX

Distributed in the USA and Canada
by Independent Publishers Group
814 North Franklin Street
Chicago, IL 60610
USA
www.ipgbooks.com

ISBN: 978-1-910392-25-6

Enitharmon Press gratefully acknowledges the financial support of
Arts Council England, through Grants for the Arts.

British Library Cataloguing-in-Publication Data.
A catalogue record for this book is available
from the British Library.

Designed in Albertina by Libanus Press
and printed in England by
Short Run Press

In memory of Michael Sheringham

CONTENTS

Introduction

Une vie n'est que cela : par là, quelqu'un fut de passage.
Imaginer Orphée, loin des montagnes thraces, se perdant dans
la neige, suivi d'un long cortège de bêtes et d'arbres glacés.
Toujours, un homme qui ne va nulle part marche sur la route.

A life is just that: someone was right there, briefly.
Imagine Orpheus, far from the Thracian mountains, becoming
lost in the snow, behind him a long cortege of animals and frozen
trees. Always, a man going nowhere is walking upon the road.

(Jean-Michel Maulpoix / Michael Bishop)

Tu voulais photographier la nuit. Tu voyais le haut des arbres se
détacher sur le ciel et c'était comme les dents d'une scie. Tu as tiré au
hasard, lancé tes mains vers l'acier dur et froid qui coupait le ciel.
Tu as pensé : « il n'y a plus rien entre Dieu et nous ».

You wanted to photograph the night. You saw the tree-tops in
relief against the sky like saw teeth. You shot at random, threw up
your hands toward the hard and cold steel which cut the sky.
You thought: "there is nothing between God and us."

(Jean-Marie Gleize / Joshua Clover, Abigail Lang and Bonnie Roy)

This anthology presents some of the vibrant and diverse voices populating French poetic practice of the last twenty years. Few of the writers are as yet well known in the Anglophone world, and some are still emerging into the French poetic scene. All were born after 1945, some began publishing only after 2000, and the majority of the texts can be described as belonging to *l'extrême contemporain* (extreme contemporary). The poets are not associated with organised schools, although the influence of earlier directions in French poetry can, of course, be identified. Since the end of the nineteenth century, poetry in French could be said to have been engaged above all in questioning its own processes, and this had led to accusations of hermeticism and detachment from ordinary concerns. In these early years of the twenty-first century, though, reflection on poetry's methods is always in the service of finding out what change poetry can effect, or how creative writing can best express and answer the urgent question of how to live in the contemporary world.

The range of responses from the contemporary French scene is broad, from the metaphysical reflections exemplified by Jean-Michel Maulpoix to experimentation with the mechanics of language. In 1995 Pierre Alferi and Olivier Cadiot published the first issue of their journal *Revue de littérature générale* (General Literary Review), which was entitled *Mécanique lyrique* (Lyrical Mechanics – or Mechanical Lyricism). The review famously refused the distinction between method, order and process on the one hand, and lyrical self-expression or inspiration on the other. Anne Portugal's *Définitif bob* is one of the most renowned manifestations of 'mechanical lyricism': the protagonist 'bob' corresponds in an indeterminate way both to a film or video-game character and to the spectator, and the text brings together elements of everyday experience whilst experimenting with the limits of a poetic text. Her work is one of those that demonstrates how irony and humour can be essential to reflect on our relationship with power structures and contemporary media. Pierre Alferi's texts, illustrated here by the opening section from *Sentimentale journée* (Night and Day), are in constant dialogue with cinema, either formally, as in his experimentation with the genre of the cine-poem, or via more direct references, such as *Gone with the Wind* in the text presented here. This extract proceeds in seemingly everyday conversational fragments, reminding us of

Guillaume Apollinaire's 'Les Fenêtres' (Windows), where the real surges into the space of the poem in a similar way, although neither poetic text makes the real any easier to comprehend.

The division refused by Alferi and Cadiot had dominated discussion of French poetry in the second half of the twentieth century, writers being classified according to whether their poetry looked for a means to account for all that appeared to be beyond language, or, alternatively, rejected the notion of a special poetic idiom. Both approaches were philosophically grounded, influenced respectively by Heidegger's interpretation of German Romantic poet Friedrich Hölderlin and by Wittgenstein's linguistic investigations. The term 'lyricism' had long been rejected by Modernist writers who no longer considered poetry to be about self-expression but rather to be the means by which the self was constructed. It was then reclaimed in the 1980s as 'nouveau lyrisme' (new lyricism) for poetic writing, such as that published and promoted by poet, publisher, and teacher Jean-Michel Maulpoix, that emphasised voice and considered itself to be an offering or gift. In contrast, the 'littéraliste' (literalist) approach that also emerged in the 1980s insisted that no particular register could lay claim to be more 'poetic' than another. It was political in its anti-elitism and insistence on the everyday language spoken by ordinary people. Texts were often produced by reusing fragments of other documents from within and outside literature. Writer, publisher, and teacher Jean-Marie Gleize is a key proponent of 'littéralité'. His volume cited at the beginning of this introduction, and from which the extracts published here are taken, is a response to the Tarnac affair of 2008–09, when the French government stormed what they called an 'anarcho-autonomist cell', a group who had set up a shop in the small village of Tarnac in central France, and kept the presumed leader under 'preventative arrest' for six months. Gleize's text combines information about this and other events with political and personal reflection.

Poetic writing need not have an explicit political impetus or object to be politically engaged or avant-garde, and others included here aim at subverting codified ways of speaking, writing and thinking through linguistic experimentation. The Italian poet and critic Alessandro De Francesco writes: 'la poésie subvertit les codes langagiers et grammaticaux, la poésie subvertit le langage de la propagande et le détournement de l'information, la poésie subvertit la représentation à la fois en tant que dédoublement du réel et en tant que figement d'identités raciales, psychologiques, sociales etc.' (*Continuum* (Uitgeverij, 2016), p. 131) (poetry subverts linguistic and grammatical codes, poetry subverts the language of propaganda and 'spin', poetry subverts representation understood both as a doubling of what is real and as the fixing of racial, psychological, social and other identities.) Or, as expressed by Christian Prigent (translated by Jérôme Game), who has been working in this way throughout his writing career:

What does it mean
'simplify poetry'?

First:
From between your teeth
drop some fartsy,
some skedaddled streamlined,
in carry-on pimped
soyme fing that gives the slack
the sack,
the submission to all

Prigent's translator Game is himself experimental in works that cannot be anthologised here because their effect stems from the stuttering live performances that he gives, 'readings' that disrupt words as they emerge. Many of the poets included in this volume are creating poetic texts which migrate throughout other fields, genres and media, potentially redefining notions of the poetic. Exciting interdisciplinary and collaborative work by Pierre Alferi, Anne-James Chaton, Jérôme Game, and Sabine Macher with musicians, visual artists (including installation and video art), choreographers, and film-makers challenges the text-bound nature of the printed poem and revives an interest in live performance. Indeed, performance is a key element of much contemporary practice, which is not always separable from music, and takes its inspiration from the performance poets of the 1960s and 70s. Anne-James Chaton is one such performer, but the text reproduced here is rather one of 'cut-up' as fragments of pre-existing texts are reused to playful, inventive effect, akin to that of Game in his performative rewritings of elements of experimental and mainstream films. Sandra Moussempès's *Sunny Girls* is also in dialogue with film, music and the everyday. Her strongly autobiographical poetic writing disrupts conventional imagery, including in particular clichés about the feminine, through the creation of a troubling environment inspired by sensations of déjà vu. Experimenting with the genre of the thriller, this text asks us: what lies behind the easy-going façade of the archetypal Californian sunny girl, if not something darker, more disturbing?

Jean-Michel Espitallier's deceptively mechanical 'Histoires de jusqu'à 15' reveals that apparently logical structures such as numbered lists conceal arbitrary categories, and demonstrate a loss of control of language. A drummer as well as a poet, Espitallier makes rhythm central not only to his performances but also to his poetry published in book form. Taking an otherwise very different starting point from the 'mechanical' approach, Philippe Beck's poem 'Mots gelés' is also linguistically experimental while reusing a previously existing text, on this occasion an episode from sixteenth-century writer François Rabelais's *Le Quart livre*. Beck's writing is characterised by neologism, subverted grammatical categories, periphrasis, personification, and reference to literary texts and historical figures. He also explores how verse and rhythm can function in the post free-verse era, frequently choosing to write lines with an odd number of syllables, in contrast to the accepted forms of classical verse.

Beck writes theoretically on another debate that has dominated French poetry since the mid-nineteenth century: the role and capacities of verse and prose. It is striking that lyrical works are now often composed in prose form, and the reflective pace of Béatrice Bonhomme's 'Visage du Fayoum', for instance, is determined by its prose rhythms as well as by its patient examination of a visual phenomenon, memory, and time. Her writing explores joy and mourning, birth and death, desire and nature.

The natural world has been at the heart of much poetic work since the 1950s, in reaction to the marvellous arbitrary images of the Surrealists. Settings such as that of the solitary traveller evoked by Maulpoix are frequent. His work aims at evoking the passage of a life, aware that words will be unable to do justice to that, but attempting nevertheless to bring to the fore the distinction, and connection, between the finitude represented by a single human life and our sense of the infinite. An alternative exploration of human experience does not require a 'poetic' landscape, as amply shown in the thoughtful attention paid by Gilles Ortlieb to sights and moments experienced, often in urban settings, in the course of an unremarkable day. He notes in particular the presence of words all around: the names of railway stations, shop signs, street names, or, in one of the poems included here, titles of books in the domestic interior. Ortlieb's work was also included in the anthology edited and translated by Jennie Feldman and Stephen Romer, *Into the Deep Street*, which brought attention to those French writers who could be considered closest to the English poetic tradition.

The city increasingly features as a central character in French poetic writing, as in Michèle Métail's pared-down poems of Berlin, which provide visual snapshots that evoke both a single experience on a given day and more generalizable responses to the city. Métail is a former member of the OuLiPo group, which adopts constraints to structure texts, and these poems are made up of ten lines of fifteen letters each, suggesting the dimensions of a 10 × 15 cm photograph. Clearly such texts pose particular challenges for the translator.

Stéphane Bouquet establishes an urban backdrop to his arresting evocations of sexual encounters and relationships, and a cast of characters interacts with the speaking subject. Oscarine Bosquet produces a sense of terrible immediacy and intimacy in the family trauma of *Mum is Down*, where fairy tales become a means of engaging with an unspeakable loss. A broader political urgency appears in *Present participle*, presented through the figure of Rosa Luxemburg. The body is both the site of performance for Sabine Macher, and a means of investigating the connections between language(s), the tongue, eating, and family relationships in 'Langue Étrangère' (Foreign Tongue). For Nathalie Quintane the body is the subject of a detached, intense, investigation of cognition, or of the link between body and mind, as she discusses the action of tying her shoelaces and taking note of the thoughts that do or do not cross her mind as she does so. Quintane exemplifies, with Christophe Tarkos, the post-1995 *Revue de littérature générale* generation. Both aim to create a type of down-to-earth 'écriture plate' (flat writing) from which any sentiment, lyricism or sense of inner self have been emptied out. Tarkos's writing glides along the surface, repeating itself in simple, but strange structures which through their intensity seem to bring us closer to the real. Tarkos died in 2004 at the age of 40 and his loss is still felt by the literary scene in France: his work continues to be edited and published posthumously. The extracts that feature in this anthology are from a volume edited by Christian Prigent in 2008.

Frank Smith and Christophe Fauchon, editors of an extensive French-language anthology of contemporary poetry, write of 'l'extraordinaire pouvoir de convocation critique du réel qui est le propre de la poésie' (*Poé/tri : 40 voix de poésie contemporaine* (Autrement, 2001), p. 8) (poetry's extraordinary ability to evoke and critique the real). We consider this to be the link between the practitioners presented here. Like the generation of poets preceding them, who, in their different ways, all rejected the dominance of the image at the heart of Surrealism, these writers demonstrate the rich variety of forms that engagement with the 'real' can take. A focus on the natural world or the urban landscape firmly anchors some pieces in their everyday surroundings. Alternatively, it allows them a means to see the finitude of human life in contrast to the environment that will survive them. From a very different perspective, texts that incorporate fragments of real documents – filmic or textual – into their fabric blur the distinction between the subject of a piece of writing and the creative response that it produces. Writing that aims at being 'flat', or neutral, is to be taken at face value rather than approached as a window onto an interpretation of the world. Some texts act as political intervention in the world, refusing the distinction between reflection and action as they do between 'poetic' and everyday language. Experiments with verse form remake language in order to produce new verbal or rhythmic utterances. It is always important for these writers to 'make' rather than to represent the real.

The original French texts we have chosen appeared with eleven different publishers, from the established Gallimard, Seuil, Champ Vallon, Flammarion and Mercure de France, through P.O.L, which has an increasing profile and is represented five times here, to lesser known small houses Al Dante – a key reference for avant-garde writing – Le temps qu'il fait, l'Attente, Le Bleu du ciel, and Tarabuste. The state of poetry publishing and distribution is often lamented, as is the purported conservatism of the big houses, but poetry is nevertheless well supported by dedicated, imaginative and ambitious individuals as well as institutionally in prizes and via the Centre National du Livre. Small magazines and journals are key to the dissemination of poetry, and the individuals whose work is included here have also been active as editors of journals such as the previously mentioned *Revue de littérature générale* (Alferi), as well as *Nioques* (Gleize), *Le Nouveau recueil* (Maulpoix), *Java* (Espitallier), *Quaderno* (Beck), *RR* (Quintane, Tarkos), *Nu(e)* (Bonhomme) and *TXT* (Prigent). The Centre international de poésie *Marseille*, a library and events centre housed in the historic Panier district, does much to promote poetry through public readings and exhibitions. In Great Britain, the Institut Français in London, the Maison Française in Oxford, and Trinity College, Cambridge, have been among the most active hosts of French poets and their translators in recent years.

It was a deliberate choice to include a significant number of female writers in this anthology. In France the reluctance of female writers to describe themselves in terms of their gender and resistance to being homogenised as 'women poets' has been matched by the entrenched preference of editors for male voices, and very few women have been included in recent French-language anthologies.

Each poet is represented here by several pages, usually, but not always, continuous or selected from a single volume. Very few poets now produce texts in the form of a single page of verse. The relatively small number of writers it has therefore been possible to include meant that we decided to restrict the selection to poets who live or have lived in France and are published by French houses. Their work can be understood in relation to the tendencies and conflicts set out above, and extending the scope to the francophone world would not have been possible without omitting work from several francophone areas. That does not mean that all the poets have always lived in France or have only French origins, although all write in French. Gilles Ortlieb, for instance, was born in Morocco and has lived in Belgium, France and Luxembourg; Sabine Macher was born in West Germany; Béatrice Bonhomme was born in Algeria; Jérôme Game has lived and worked in Britain and the USA, and Anne-James Chaton in the Netherlands.

Connections between French and American poetry are well-established. The Objectivists, for example, have been an important influence on poets working in France, who have also translated their work into French. Links between French and British poetry are fewer and more tenuous, however. The Cambridge Conference of Contemporary Poetry did bring together young avant-garde poets from both sides of the Channel, during the 1990s in particular, but otherwise invitations to French poets to read or perform work in the UK remain occasional. This anthology aims at bringing a range of recent voices to the notice of a readership based above all in the United Kingdom, although the twenty translators have lived and worked across Europe, North America and beyond. Just over half of the translations have been previously published, generally in journals or other publications with a small circulation; the texts by Alferi, Bosquet, Gleize, and Portugal appeared in translated single-authored volumes. As a result, no single translation approach dominates, but the presentation of the texts on facing pages is intended to enable comparison between French and English versions, and to encourage the reader with knowledge of French to seek out further publications in the original language.

The editors are grateful to Peter Target for his advice and assistance, and for the guidance offered by Stephen Romer, and by Eric Giraud from the Centre International de poésie *Marseille*. We would like to thank Andrew Rothwell, who contributed to the translation of Philippe Beck's 'Mots gelés', as well as the authors and translators who generously agreed to the inclusion of their texts, and especially those who have provided new translations: Barbara Beck, Michael Bishop, Jérôme Game and Eléna Rivera.

Note Asterisks indicate that the selection skips pages of the original text.

CHRISTIAN PRIGENT

extracts from *Ecrit au Couteau* (Paris, P.O.L., 1993)

bref sur la méthode

1

Numérote tes abattis !
change de viande !

(me dis-je)

Et en même temps :

Simplifie la poésie !

CHRISTIAN PRIGENT

extracts from *Ecrit au Couteau*, translated by Jérôme Game
(revised version of text published in *Hollow Life – Selection, translation, and presentation of Christian Prigent* (CCCP Press, Cambridge, 2001))

brief on the method

1

Get ready! You're in for it!
change meat!

(I tell myself)

And all at once:

Simplify poetry!

2

Qu'est-ce que cela signifie
« simplifie la poésie » ?

Premièrement :

D'entre tes dents
lâche du pétant,
du caréné carapaté,
en maqué mic-mac
cake chiose qui saque
le mou,
la soumission à tout !

Deuxièmement :

Zappe l'halluciné dit spiritualité !
Raidis-toi du gosier !
Va au creux de ton cru nervé !
Trouve le trou où t'as peur de tout !
Calcine tes boues !
Debout !

2

What does it mean
'simplify poetry'?

First:

From between your teeth
drop some fartsy,
some skedaddled streamlined,
in carry-on pimped
soyme fing that gives the slack
the sack,
the submission to all

Second:

Zap the hallucinated said spirituality!
Stiffen from the throat!
Go to the hollow of your nerved out raw!
Find the hole where you're scared of all!
Scorch your muds!
Get up!

Troisièmement :

Axe !
Axe !

Lance du son dans l'air !
Stocke un bloc qu'était pas là !
Sculpte ça :
totem d'ego
cale du vertigo !

Danse !
Condense !
Accélère !
Ich und Er
Dichter ! :

Rien à dire que ça :
né, nié
je suis là
voyez mon tas :

moi est ce trou d'émoi dans ce qui est là.

Third:

Axis!
Axis!

Throw some sound ' n the air!
Stock a block that wasn't there!
Sculpt that:
totem of ego
wedge some vertigo!

Dance!
Condense!
Accelerate,
Ich und Er,
Dichter!:

Nothing to say but that:
born, denied,
I am there,
see my pile:

me is this hole of emotion in what is there.

3

Car le savoir est très épais,
sa queue est vraiment grosse
pour le tendre trou d' la po
ésie.

Et si
– I did say yes
O, at lightning and lashed rod ! –
elle en crevait,
Apollon, *das*
Athletische des südlichen Menschen
sous l'arcobaleno
avec ton corset rococo :

« c'est mon corps baleiné,
dit l'poète,
hard down with a
horror of height,
qui s'arque,
von Göttern
geschlagen,
troussé sous sa gaine,

avec en rêve un petit con en strass ».

3

For knowledge is very thick,
its cock is really big
for the tender hole of po
etry.

And if
– I did say yes
O, at lightning and lashed rod! –
she was dying of it,
Apollo *(das*
Athletische des südlichen Menschen)
under the arcobaleno
with your rococo corset:

'it's my boned body,
says th'poet,
hard down with
a horror of height,
that curves,
von Göttern
geschlagen,
tucked up 'der his girdle,

with in a dream a little strass cunt'.

NATHALIE QUINTANE

Chaussure (Paris: P.O.L., 1997)

Lacer des chaussures est une chose que je peux faire yeux fermés (ou dans une pièce obscure).

Je peux très bien lacer mes chaussures en ne pensant à rien d'autre.

Cependant, si, dès le réveil, un air de musique m'a poursuivie (j'ai continué à le chanter "intérieurement" quelles que soient mes activités), j'aurais bien plus de difficultés à lacer mes chaussures sans poursuivre ma chanson, ou, sans, à la fois, poursuivre ma chanson et déplorer qu'elle me poursuive.

Heureusement, le plus souvent, le laçage de mes chaussures me permet de penser à autre chose, et ainsi, de gagner du temps. J'ai, simultanément, un geste et une pensée très éloignés l'un de l'autre.

Comme je profite pleinement de cette possibilité – depuis que je suis en âge de lacer mes chaussures sans y penser –, je dois, à présent, faire de gros efforts pour ne pas penser à autre chose tandis que je lace mes chaussures. J'y parviens parfois en décomposant les mouvements, ou en observant le cuir, ou les caractéristiques du lacet.

NATHALIE QUINTANE

Chaussure, translated by Macgregor Card for *The Germ* #5 (2001)

Tying my shoes is something I can do eyes shut (or in a dark room).

I can tie my shoes just fine while thinking of nothing else.

Still, if, since waking up, I can't shake a piece of music (I go on singing it "internally" whatever I'm doing), I'll have considerable trouble tying my shoes without continuing my little song, or, without, all at once, continuing my song and cursing it for haunting me.

Fortunately, more often, the tying of my shoes allows me to think of other things, and in this way, to make up time. I have, simultaneously, a gesture and a thought quite autonomous from one another.

As I clearly benefit from this potential – ever since I've been old enough to tie my shoes without thinking of shoe-tying – I must, presently, make great strides to not think of other things while tying my shoes. I succeed now and again by analysing the shoe's motions, or observing the leather, or characteristics of the lace.

Je suis à présent presque incapable de ne faire que lacer mes chaussures.

Je ne me souviens d'aucune pensée originale que me soit venue en laçant mes chaussures.

La plupart du temps, je répète la liste des tâches qu'il me reste à accomplir, liste que je connais depuis le matin, ou depuis la veille ; ou je ressasse une pensée contrariante.

En revanche, en marchant, il m'arrive parfois de faire des découvertes intéressantes.

Sans doute la position penchée (le sang monte plus vite au cerveau ? le ventre comprimé par les cuisses ?) ne favorise-t-elle pas l'activité intellectuelle.

Et pourtant, je ne suis pas vraiment préoccupée par cette incapacité, laçant mes chaussures, soit de penser à quelque chose d'intéressant, soit de ne penser à rien.

J'imagine que des occasions plus favorables se présentent dans la journée.

I am presently almost incapable of only tying my shoes.

I can't remember one original thought which came to me while tying my shoes.

Most of the time, I rehearse the list of chores that remain to be completed, a list that I will have known since morning, or the day before, or else I scrutinize a prickly thought.

In return, it sometimes happens that, walking on my way, I'll make interesting discoveries.

Undoubtedly, bending over (blood rushes quickly to the head? the stomach compressed by the thighs?) does not facilitate intellectual activity.

Nevertheless, I am not overly concerned with this incapacity, when tying my shoes, either to think of something interesting, or think of nothing at all.

I believe that the best opportunities present themselves in daylight.

Je me vois, ayant appris à n'avoir une activité intellectuelle qu'au moment où je lace mes chaussures. Chaque fois que je les lace, une foule de propositions me vient à l'esprit, que je note aussitôt – notes prises, je déferais mes lacets, que je referais illico, pour entraîner de nouvelles idées.
J'aurais appris à les lacer lentement.
Naîtraient peut-être des pensées propres au laçage des chaussures, une pensée suivant les cinq étapes : 1. Je tire les lacets. 2. Je passe l'extrémité de l'un dans l'autre. 3. Je fais une première boucle. 4. J'en fais en seconde et 5. Je serre.

Quand la rosette est presque terminée, je fais attention de bien la serrer, afin qu'elle ne se défasse pas.

I see myself, having learned to undertake intellectual activity only at the moment of shoe-tying. Every time I tie my shoes, a flurry of propositions occur to me, which I duly note – having taken note, I undo the laces, which I will redo forthwith, to encourage new ideas.
I will have learned to tie them slowly.
Perhaps the ideas proper to shoe-tying will come about as such, a thought process following the five stages: 1. I draw up the laces. 2. I pass the tip of one over the next. 3. I tie the first bow. 4. I tie a second and 5. I tighten.

When the bow is almost finished, I make sure to pull it tight, so that it won't come undone.

Aussi loin que soient mes talons de mon cerveau, des terminaisons nerveuses, via le corps, relient directement les premiers au second : mon talon est dans mon cerveau, et inversement. Or, le talon de ma chaussure, qui est un prolongement de celui du pied, le renforçant et le protégeant, siège donc aussi dans mon cerveau.

La chaussure n'est pas un "second" pied, mais – et je le perçois au terme d'une longue marche, quand j'ai la sensation que je ne puis ôter mes chaussures sans ôter mes pieds – est le pied, et comme tel, monte au cerveau.

As long as my heels are part of my brain, nerve endings, throughout the body, connect the former directly to the latter: my heel is in my head, and vice-versa. Now, the heel of my shoe, which extends from that of my foot, reinforcing and protecting it, also resides in my brain.

The shoe is not a "second" foot, but – and I notice this during a long walk, when overcome by a sensation that I cannot remove my shoes without also removing my feet – is the foot, and as such, hails from the brain.

PIERRE ALFERI

Sentimentale journée (Paris: P.O.L, 1997)

VOUS ÊTES INVITÉS

La journée s'avance masquée
La sensation, la plus forte et la plus subtile
De l'aujourd'hui
La nuit
On y voit nus les rouages
L'encombrement du temps
On fait eau, on va droit
Sur l'iceberg.

Et la journée s'avance masquée
Sur des rails trop étroits. Décidément
Elle ne fait pas son âge, ce qui ne veut pas dire
Qu'elle est plus vieille. S'il suffisait de tendre
Une petite glace en direction de la lumière trop forte
Pour y lire à l'envers – quoi ? Pas la vérité
Tout de même. Simplement le kilo de tomates
Pèse un peu plus ou un peu moins. La rumeur
De la ville tend la perche de minute en minute
À la journée dans son chorus qui paraît frêle
Par des riffs de cuivres huilés. L'arrangement
Sent la sueur et le big band en smokings pathétiques
Imite un orchestre classique. – Si si, cette cotte de mailles
Vous va, je vous jure, à ravir. – Je ne dis pas

PIERRE ALFERI

night and day, translated by Kate Lermitte Campbell
(Iowa City & Paris: La Presse, 2012)

YOU ARE INVITED

The day advances masked
The strongest subtlest feeling
Of the day
The night
Lays its mechanisms bare
The burden of time
Water's coming in, we're heading straight
For the iceberg.

So the day advances masked
On very narrow rails. Oh no,
It doesn't look its age, which doesn't mean
It's older. Were it enough to hold
A mirror to the overbearing light
To read back to front across it – what? Not the truth
All the same. Just that the kilo of tomatoes
Weighs a bit more or less. The hum
Of the town directs the boom from one minute to the next
Following the day's chorus, frail-sounding
Through riffs of oiled brass. The rendition
Smells of sweat and the big band in ragged tails
Mocks a classical orchestra. – No, no, that coat of mail
Couldn't suit you better, I swear. – I'm not saying

Qu'elle jure, mais si on danse ? Votre voisin de table
Trouve la musique pas assez actuelle, il lit
Les magazines. – Alors dans trois ans tu n'aimeras
Plus ce que tu aimes aujourd'hui. – Non
Ce n'est pas si simple. J'aime, dit le voisin, ce qui me donne
La sensation, la plus forte et la plus subtile,
Comme un parfum traverse la salle sur des talons
Aiguilles, de l'aujourd'hui. Plus tard
Quand je ferai sauter le bouchon je sais
(Et ce savoir ajoute une tuile à mon plaisir
Un peu vert pour l'instant) qu'elle sera là
Millésimée. – Je vois. Ce genre de chose ne m'arrive
Jamais, j'en ai peur, ou par la grâce de créatures
Désespérément vaporeuses. L'eau qui bout juste
Avant son ascension dans la cafetière, le soleil
Quand il s'épand sur la moquette d'une propreté douteuse
La fourchette qui tintait contre l'étain
D'une boîte d'abats pour le chat le rend dingue.
Par exemple. Et cela, vous voyez, n'a pas grand-chose à voir
Avec la culture. Je ne lis plus. En tout cas
Plus dans l'espoir de me sentir – comment ? sentir
Tout court. Il y a des gens qui mettent leurs polaroïds
Au freezer ; ils vieillissent mal, c'est notoire, mais
Ne prenez pas pour un désir de retarder l'effacement
Celui de couleurs irréelles. Iceberg, aurores boréales.
Le temps ne coule incolore qu'à température
Ambiante. Dès que l'atmosphère coagule
Ça pue l'huile de cuisson. Le lave-vaisselle a fait
De fines croûtes étranges comme des fragments de météore
Avec des restes plus humains. Il y a des jours

It clashes, but what if we dance? The man next to you
Doesn't find the music modern enough, he's a magazine
Reader. – So in three years you'll no longer love
The things you love today. – No
It's not that simple. I like, says your neighbor, things that give me
The strongest subtlest feeling
Like a perfume crossing the room on stiletto
Heels, of the day. Later
When I pop the cork I know
(And this adds spice to my pleasure
A bit bland as yet) that it'll be there
Vintage. – I see. That sort of thing never happens
To me I'm afraid, or only thanks to desperately
Vaporous creatures. Water that boils just
Before rising in the coffee pot, the sun
When it spills over the stained carpet
The fork clinking against the pewter
Of a plate of scraps for the cat drives him nuts.
For example. And that, you see, doesn't have much to do
With culture. I no longer read. Well
No longer hoping to feel – what? To feel
Quite simply. Some people put their polaroids
In the freezer; they age badly, that's obvious, but
Don't mistake the desire to postpone effacement
For that of unreal colors. Iceberg, aurora borealis.
Time only flows colorless at room
Temperature. As soon as the atmosphere coagulates
It stinks of cooking oil. The dishwasher has made
Thin scales as strange as fragments of meteorite
With more human remains. There are days

Comme ça. Pour celui-ci ce sera tout
D'accord ? D'ailleurs la lumière soudain baisse
Dans le bar, signal du changement de tarif
Et l'heure d'été, une belle arnaque, blanchit
Le larcin du soir en taxant le sommeil du matin.
- Bonne nuit, dors bien mon amour. – Si c'est un ordre
Sache que je vais me mutiner. Le capitaine est à fond de cale.
Dans cette mélasse une chatte ne retrouverait pas ses petits
Et le port de départ ni celui vers quoi nous voguons
N'est en vue. Hier m'a posé un lapin. Demain
Demain (*Autant en emporte le vent*)
Est un autre jour. La nuit, quelle violence
Inouïe, tu ne trouves pas ? Tu dors.
Non qu'elle évoque la mort, la solitude hantée
Des enfants – ces pensées peupleraient l'insomnie –
Mais on y voit nus les rouages de la veille.
Sur le pont l'océan tout entier se change
En salle des machines et dans chaque tour de garde
La discontinuité amorphe des heures soumet
La mousse à la torture. S'il avait su ! Pas une angoisse
Intéressante, une à la Heidegger, comme dit
Cet ami qui ne dort plus : un bazar, un medley sadique
Des plus mauvaises chansons sur Radio Nostalgie,
L'encombrement du temps. Comprends-tu que l'on ait
Bien envie de te réveiller, mon amour, de secouer
Tes épaules pour te montrer ce qui se passe d'affreux ?
- Qu'est-ce qu'il y a ? – On fait eau, on va droit
Sur l'iceberg, et non, il n'y a rien à l'horizon, c'est bien
Ce qui affole. Le *Titanic*, selon certaines sources,
N'aurait jamais coulé mais un autre navire

Like that. That'll be enough for this one
OK? Anyway the light is falling suddenly
In the bar, signaling a change of tariff
And daylight saving time, what a con, launders
Evening's loot by taxing morning sleep.
- Good night, sleep well my love. – If that's an order
Rest assured I'll mutiny. The captain's at the back of the hold.
A cat couldn't find her kittens in this murk
And neither the port we left nor the one we're heading for
Is visible. Yesterday stood me up. Tomorrow
Tomorrow (*Gone with the wind*)
Is another day. Night-time, what unexpected
Violence, don't you think? You're sleeping.
Not that it evokes death, the haunted solitude
Of children – these thoughts will populate insomnia –
But it lays yesterday's mechanisms bare
On the deck the whole ocean transforms itself
Into a machine room and at each lookout post
The amorphous discontinuity of hours tortures
The ship's boy. If only he'd known! Not an interesting
Angst, Heidegger-style, as
That sleep-deprived friend says: a shambles, a sadistic medley
Of the worst songs on Golden Oldies AM,
The burden of time. Do you see that someone
Longs to wake you, my love, to grasp
Your shoulders to show you the dreadful things going on
- What is it? – There's water coming in, we're heading straight
For the iceberg, and no, there's nothing on the horizon, that's just
The horror of it. Some say the *Titanic*
Never sank, but another

Presque identique auquel des armateurs véreux
Auraient donné son nom, comptant sur un naufrage sans morts
Pour encaisser la prime. Le *Titanic* – le vrai –
Mouillerait encore dans une rade paisible
On ne sait où. Il existe une carte postale
Montrant un paquebot à demi englouti – le *Cabiria*
Ou bien le *Caribbean* – et cette légende en gras :
« Vous êtes invités. » Il s'agissait de l'inauguration
D'un restaurant. Longtemps j'ai cherché à qui l'envoyer,
Une femme certainement. J'avoue que je m'identifie
Assez à ce bateau débaptisé privé de son big band
Qui a coulé, coule encore dans nos têtes et
N'a pas coulé. Surtout le soir : le soir
Est si sentimental. J'ai toujours cette carte.
Tu l'as gagnée à la sueur de ton sommeil.

Almost identical ship; that its corrupt owner
Sold its name, counting on a shipwreck with no dead
To cash in on the insurance. The *Titanic* – the real one –
Would still be anchored in some peaceful harbor
No one knows where. A postcard exists
Showing a half-sunk steamship – the *Cabiria*
Or perhaps the *Caribbean* – with this caption in bold:
'You are invited.' It had something to do with the inauguration
Of a restaurant, I wondered who to send it to for ages,
Definitely a woman. I admit that I feel quite an affinity
With this renamed boat stripped of its big band
That sank, sinks still in our minds and
Never sank. Most often in the evening: evenings
Are so sentimental. I still have that card.
You've earned it through the toil of your sleep.

MICHÈLE MÉTAIL

Toponyme: Berlin (St Benoit du Sault : Tarabuste, 2002)

LA VILLE, DE LA VILLE
(plan parcellaire)

effeuillé d'hiver
se dresse là entre
des murs, triangle
angles sombres où
s'étagent à mi-bois
des rameaux épais
quand aux pointes
un bourgeon fendu
jour, jour suivant
éclose l'éclosion

12 avril 2000 : marronnier dans la cour

*

à claque mur, murée
s'y vrille la vigne
vierge et support
de couvrir, loggia
où l'abandon à demi
un fauteuil, tendu
tendant sur la rue
réfractée, l'image
de l'usure si vraie
à s'user tout à fait

9 mai 2000 : Potsdam.Villa à vendre

*

MICHÈLE MÉTAIL

Toponyme: Berlin, translated by Susan Wicks

THE CITY, FROM THE CITY
(a town plan in plots)

winter leafless
rising up between
walls, a triangle
dark angles where
thick branches are
tiers at mid-growth
when up at the tips
one bud has split
one day to the next
its bursting burst

12 April 2000: chestnut-tree in the courtyard

*

walled up, walled in
the twisting vine
virgin over canes
veils lean-to glass
a half-abandoned
armchair strains
towards the street
refracted, image
of outwear so true
it wears it through

9 May 2000: Potsdam, villa for sale

*

motif de symétrie
aux perspectives
la percée urbaine
déjà monumentale
axe et rectiligne
carcan quadrillé
de la parade, stucs
allée où triomphe
inattendu, si doux
un parfum, tilleul

18 juin 2000 : Karl Marx Allee

*

scandés, percutés
aux corps, des sons
les graves, rythme
dans le mouvement
de répéter, marqué
sur une pulsation
à faire et refaire
ceci, la vie l'envie
du monde, un projet
échoué drôlement

8 juillet 2000 : Love Parade, Tiergarten

*

motif of symmetry
in the long views
spread of the city
today monumental
axis and unbending
squared-off showy
shackles, stuccoes
triumphal avenue
for the triumph of
sweet scent of lime

18 June 2000: Karl Marx Allee

*

rhythmic, beating
in our bodies, sounds
the deep ones, beat
inside the motion
of repeating, marked
with a pulsation
doing and redoing
this, aspire, desire
the world, a plan
that faltered oddly

8 July 2000: Love Parade, Tiergarten

*

voûtes et rosaces
un portique, ruine
laissée vide hors
d'un pigeon, fiente
lignes blanchies
de la destination
dévoyée des voies
égarée autrement
la gare terrassée
son terminus vain

13 août 2000 : Porticus Anhalter Bahnhof
Portique de l'ancienne gare d' Anhalt

*

reflet de cristal
la nuit, la coupole
enflammée des ors
désormais hantée
nausée, l'histoire
ressasse rôdeuse
tandis qu'un signe
pour que s'ébranle
même chancelante
si lente la marche

9 novembre 2000 : manifestation contre
le racisme devant la synagogue. Oranienburgstrasse

*

arches rose window
portico, a ruin left
cleared out apart
from a pigeon, shit
the whitened lines
of destination now
have wandered off
derailed, a station
dead in its tracks
a pointless terminus

13 August 2000: Porticus Anhalter Bahnhof
Portico, old Anhalt station.

*

glint of crystal
night, the cupola
aflame with gold
haunted from now on
a sickness, restless
history chews over
while at a signal
for the march to go
or even totter, such
a gradual advance

9 November 2000: anti-racist demonstration
in front of the synagogue, Oranienburgstrasse.

*

en affiches la vie
placardée de joie
si facile, si douce
où défile une rame
s'arrête et change
alors d'un couloir
langueur des sons
comme l'accordéon
la voix obsédante
seule sa solitude

10 janvier 2001 : un musicien russe à la
station de métro Heidelbergerplatz

*

neige, tard de l'est
qui couvre encore
au sol et marquage
les files à suivre
sans voir des rues
effacées, signaux
où tourner, cadran
écoulé aux heures
libre ni interdit
pour penser à l'été

25 mars 2001 : Passage à l'heure d'été.
Tempête de neige. Rathenauplatz

in posters, life
pasted in delight
so easily, so sweet
as a train winds by
to stop and change
then from a subway
come languid sounds
like an accordion
the haunting voice
of only loneliness

10 January 2001: Russian busker at
Heidelbergerplatz tube station.

*

late from the east
snow still covers
markings, ground
the lanes to follow
blind and streets
erased, a signal
where to turn, a dial
wiped of hours, free
nor against the law
to think of summer

25 March 2001: change to summer time.
Snowstorm, Rathenauplatz.

ANNE PORTUGAL

définitif bob (Paris: P.O.L, 2002)

10

Et sur quelques causes de l'état présent
valeur naufrage qui équivaut il n'a
que l'utilisation latérale d'un corps d'homme donné à la science
un 'mon petit ami' le diminutif de richard
qui n'allait pas du tout

fait-il aucun effort passer vomir
unité alcool 4 les configurations

dimanche après-midi conversation oh rien oh rien un peu vidé
aux pieds de saint jean l'esprit s'accorde bien l'appui des mains
sa dévotion

mais bob il peut comme ça officiel résister aux pressions dans
les courbes

ANNE PORTUGAL

absolute bob, translated from the French by Jennifer Moxley
(Anyart, Providence: Burning Deck, 2010)

10

And as for certain causes of the present state
value sinking which equals he has
only the sideways use of a man's body given over to science
a "my boyfriend" richard's pet name
which doesn't suit him at all

will he make no effort passing up vomiting
alcohol unit 4 the configurations

sunday afternoon conversation oh nothing oh nothing a little void
at the feet of saint john the soul allows itself the support of hands
his devotion

but that's how bob can officially resist the pressure of linebreaks

précis ne reste que promener
déterminant deux luminaires
allumés-jour désordre ou sa consolation
l'idée de ressembler certaine
le bruit moteur vers son amour plus fort
même si même si encombrement tellement fort
une aventure une occasion le film avec
ça va

ne peut l'avoir la journée d'autres lui c'est toute
en abordant cette île il n'est resté que ça
trouvée distance un plan d'elle la peinture
qui est dans l'île il n'y a pas un mot plus collectif
inventé religieux une possibilité vue avec
il avait tout sur un petit terrain pendant trois mois
très bien il fait des projections au-dehors
ça va

precisely nothing left but to take a walk
determining two floodlights
lit in daytime disorder or his consolation
the resemblance idea a sure thing
the motor noise towards his stronger love
even if even if the encumbrance is strong
an adventure an occasion the film with
it's ok

can't have a day like others for him it's all
about reaching this island it's all that remains
found the distance a map of it the painting
that is on the island there is no word more communal
more made up more religious a possibility seen in tandem
for three months he had everything on a little spot of ground
very well he shoots some footage outdoors
it's ok

et pour l'équivalent abstentionniste
déplacement posthume de
la bouche à peindre du début du parlant
il n'a scrupuleux que le ha
de hamac
et qu'il travaille à restaurer

il a mixé l'envers du mur du son
heurt dans le cadre
détonation qui possède
rapprochée
de la neige tombée de rien rideau pour regarder
longueur épais ruban la baie
sa plate-forme

car l'avion qui commence loin
dans le frais encore y est présent

and for the equivalent abstainer
posthumous dislocation of
the mouth to be painted in early soundfilms
nothing's scrupulous but the ha
of hammock
and that he works to restore

he mixed the backside of the wall of sound
collision inside the frame
explosion came closer
holding
snow which fell out of nothing a curtain to see
length thick ribbon the bay
its platform

because the airplane that starts far
in the cool air remains there

mais bob il peut comme ça pas voir le paysage
et s'envoyer radar
la fille du roi
il a vu il a vu il a vu
bref il a vu d'excellents bobinages en divisions indépendantes
ouvrir fermer les objets bougent pas
et trouver lui complètement rire
pas de quoi s'occuper
petits lézards et pas de main

but that's how bob can not see the countryside
and take radar
the king's daughter
he saw he saw he saw
in short he saw excellent reels in independent divisions
opening closing the objects don't move
and finding him totally laugh
nothing to keep him busy
little lizards and no hand

JEAN-MICHEL MAULPOIX

Pas sur la neige (Paris: Mercure de France, 2004)

Quelqu'un marcherait sur la neige, sous un ciel jaune et gris d'hiver. À pas lents, un peu lourds, qui se rapprochent ou qui s'éloignent. Juste une silhouette, enveloppée dans un manteau de laine noire. Un rudiment de signe sombre cerné par la blancheur. Allant, sans que l'on sache pourquoi, ni vers où. Devant lui, nul chemin visible. Seulement l'hiver qui tombe, recouvrant sans un bruit l'empreinte de ses pas sur la neige.

Quelqu'un marche dans le silence. Quelqu'un s'efface dans l'invisible. Sans paroles, sans parfum. Personne à côté. Parfois levant la tête. Parfois baissant les yeux. Mais c'est en lui que tombe la neige où il continue de marcher.

Neige : le nom *d'autre chose* où chaque pas s'enfonce de son poids d'énigme.

Quelqu'un aurait poussé la porte de la saison froide. Aurait fait taire son cœur. N'accordant plus guère d'importance aux péripéties de sa propre histoire. Traversant un deuil clair. Avec lenteur, éperdument.

S'en aller dans la neige, ce serait comme quitter le monde. N'être qu'un passant incertain dans l'indistinct glacé. Un point de petitesse et d'anxiété dont la tiédeur va dans le froid.

Pas sur le souvenir de la couleur perdue. Pas sur le temps. Un lumineux sommeil souhaitable dans une espèce de mort très douce. Pas sur la mémoire de l'amour, faite de petits cristaux coupants, soudés les uns aux autres. Pas où il n'est plus de chemin tracé. Pas qui vont, qui font leur chemin. Laissant derrière eux bien plus que des creux : un long collier de coques vides que le vent d'hiver emplit peu à peu.

JEAN-MICHEL MAULPOIX

Footsteps in the Snow, translated by Michael Bishop

Someone I imagine walking in the snow, beneath a yellow grey winter sky. The slow, heavy steps getting nearer or moving off. Just a silhouette, wrapped in a black woollen coat. A dark rudimentary sign surrounded by whiteness. Going forth, without it being known why, or towards what. Before him, no visible path. Only the falling winter, soundlessly covering over the imprint of his footsteps in the snow.

Someone is walking on in silence. Someone is blotted out in the invisible. Not speaking, odourless. No one alongside him. Sometimes looking up. Sometimes gazing down. But it is within himself that is falling the snow in which he carries on walking.

Snow : the name of *something else* in which each footstep sinks with its burden of enigma.

Someone has presumably pushed open the door of the cold season. Silenced his heart. Scarcely now granting significance to the ups and downs of his own story. Traversing a mournfulness lit with brightness. Slowly, bewilderedly.

Going off into the snow would be like leaving the world. Being a mere uncertain passing figure in the icy indistinctness. A dot of smallness and anxiety whose warmth moves on through the cold.

Footsteps upon the memory of lost colour. Footsteps in time. A desirable luminous slumber in a kind of most sweet death. Footsteps through love's memory made up of little sharp crystals soldered one to the other. Footsteps where there is no longer any path traced out. Footsteps that move on, making their way. Leaving behind much more than hollowed tracks: a long necklace of empty shells that the winter wind gradually fills in.

Des pas faits pour se perdre. Ou pour être perdus. Déjà de l'eau coule sous la neige. Filet d'eau ou filet de voix. Juste un peu de vie inaudible. Un peu de froidure vive : c'est de la neige qui meurt en larmes, lentement, tendrement défaite. La blancheur qui s'égoutte et retourne à la terre. Peut-être les obsèques d'une âme ayant pris froid naguère… Que sais-je ? Ce n'est que neige fondant au soleil du printemps et confondant dans la lumière la fin et le commencement. C'est comme la musique d'une prière qu'en écoutant fondre la neige on entend.

Celui qui marche sur la neige marche sur du ciel tombé. Il traverse des pays effacés, des lointains devenus très proches, et s'en retourne vers une enfance plus vaste que la sienne.

Cette neige, c'est encore de la mort et de la mémoire consumées, comme les lilas, les roses et les tulipes très rouges, comme l'enfant qui joue dans la cour, les insectes bruissant dans le pré et tout bonheur sur cette terre.

Par quels chemins dans l'invisible sont-ils passés, ces disparus qui nous reviennent ? Si décharnés, si pâles qu'on n'en voit que les pas ?

Où s'en est-il allé, celui qui a marqué la neige de son pas ? Celui dont il reste la trace, mais dont la présence a fondu ? Celui qui n'est plus qu'un creux d'homme, son empreinte dans un lit défait ?

Une vie n'est que cela : par là, quelqu'un fut de passage.

Imaginer Orphée, loin des montagnes thraces, se perdant dans la neige, suivi d'un long cortège de bêtes et d'arbres glacés. Toujours, un homme qui ne va nulle part marche sur la route.

Footsteps made to lose oneself in. Or to be themselves lost. Already water flows beneath the snow. A trickle of water or a trickle of voices. Just a little inaudible life. A little sharp coldness: it is snow dying tearfully away, slowly, tenderly undone. The whiteness that drips away and returns to the earth. Perhaps the funeral of a soul having lately caught cold… What do I know of such things? It is merely snow melting in the spring sunshine and mingling end and beginning in the light. It is like the music of a prayer that, listening to the snow melt away, one can hear.

He who is walking upon snow is walking upon fallen sky. He traverses lands erased, distant places suddenly become near, and he returns to a childhood vaster than his own.

The snow is still death and memory consumed, like lilacs, roses and really red tulips, like the child playing in the courtyard, insects humming away in the meadow and all happiness upon the earth.

Via what paths in the invisible did they pass, those who have disappeared and come back to us? Those so fleshless, so pale we can see nothing but their footsteps?

Where has he gone off to, he who has left the mark of his footsteps in the snow? He whose trace remains with us, but whose presence has melted away? He who now is but a hollow man, his imprint in an unmade bed?

A life is just that: someone was right there, briefly.

Imagine Orpheus, far from the Thracian mountains, becoming lost in the snow, behind him a long cortege of animals and frozen trees. Always, a man going nowhere is walking upon the road.

SABINE MACHER

langue étrangère, transatlantic verse 2 (2006)

je mange des choses que mes frères, surtout le deuxième, de deux ans mon ainé, n'arrivent pas à manger. c'est mon père ogre qui nous force. il est assis derrière son assiette et il arrive à tout engloutir. des couennes, des os, des lentilles, des pois cassés, du porc du porc le gras du porc, la moelle des os d'animaux sacrifiés, il suce les os, si bien habillé, en costume trois pièces et père hardi, il dévore des choses immangeables pour le plaisir de ma mère, il ogre. parfois devant lui dans l'assiette, fumant dans son jus, la longue langue d'une vache qui ne parlera plus. chez le boucher elle est horrible à voir aussi, mais cuite, c'est pire.

peut-être pas.

ce n'est pas ma langue à moi. mon père la coupe en tranches horizontales, il parle des papilles, il dit des mots pour dire la connaissance de ce qui dit les goûts, de ce qui nous dit ce que nous mangeons, de ce qui ne peut plus rien dire parce que nous allons le manger. ça a un drôle de goût, ce n'est pas gras, c'est un goût seul et mauvais. j'avale la langue, je n'en ai pas envie, mais j'arrive, ça me fait des points bonus. mon frère dégoûté ne goûte pas.

et quand c'est dedans on ne le voit plus.

je n'ai jamais senti ma langue parce qu'elle est dans ma bouche, je ne la mâche pas, je la laisse caresser le bord des dents, je la regarde, elle a des couleurs et des ronds de différentes tailles et des entailles, des plis, elle est féroce mais elle est dans ma bouche.

dans un magazine pour jeunes adolescents je lis les dix variantes du zungenkuss, le baiser de la langue. je lis qu'on met la langue dans la bouche de l'autre. c'est dangereux.

SABINE MACHER

foreign tongue, translated by Simone Forti

i eat things that my brothers, especially the second, two years my elder, can't eat. it's my ogre father who compels us. seated behind his plate, he shoves everything down his gullet. rinds, bones, lentils, split peas, pork, pork pork fat, bone marrow of sacrificed animals, he sucks the bones, well dressed, a brazen father in a three piece suit. he devours inedible things to please my mother, he ogres. at times sitting before him in its plate, steaming in its juice, the long tongue of a cow who will speak no more. already horrible to see at the butcher's, cooked, it's worse.

maybe not.

it's not my tongue, my father cuts it into horizontal slices, he talks about taste buds, says words to acknowledge that which can no longer tell us anything because we are about to eat it. it has a strange taste, not fatty, a single, bad taste. my brother, disgusted, doesn't take a taste. i swallow the tongue, i don't feel like it but i manage, i gain bonus points.

and when it's inside we don't see it any more.

i've never felt my tongue because it's in my mouth, i don't chew it, i let it caress the edges of my teeth, i look at it, it has colors, circles of different shapes, gashes and creases, it is ferocious but it's in my mouth.

in a magazine for young adolescents i read about the ten variations of the zungenkuss, the tongue kiss. i read that you put your tongue in someone's mouth. it's dangerous.

après une fête je le fais, avec une amie, annette, celle avec qui j'étais enfant aussi, je sais qu'il faut que j'ouvre la bouche pour commencer à cesser d'être un enfant, un garçon plus âgé de deux ans au moins, avec des cheveux roux, que je n'ai jamais vu avant cette fête et avec qui je suis en quattuor, lui est avec un ami, je suis avec une amie, sur une bosse de pelouse dans un quartier d'une petite ville en allemagne de l'ouest, ludwigshafen, ou tübingen, je crois que c'est tübingen, parce que l'amie habite là et que je suis avec elle, et ludwigshafen, c'est là où elle habitait avant, après avoir quitté la rue où nous sommes devenues amies, à freiburg, je ne sais plus alors que c'est simple, le garçon met sa langue dans ma bouche quand je ferme les yeux, je ne sais pas quoi faire, si, grâce à l'étude des dix variantes du baiser de la langue je sais qu'elle va venir dans ma bouche, que je peux faire des choses avec la mienne à l'approche de la sienne, mais aussi je peux juste ouvrir la bouche comme j'ai appris à le faire en jouant à mund auf augen zu et voir ce qui se passe, ferme les yeux, ouvre la bouche, une surprise arrive dans la bouche, de goût et de forme, quelque chose que je n'ai pas vu et qu'il faut que je ne connaisse qu'avec les yeux de ma langue, je peux le laisser descendre dans le fond de la gorge, là où je ne vois jamais ma langue, à moins que ce ne soit une farce et qu'il faille le recracher, on ne sait pas avec ce jeu, la langue du garçon roux, très expérimenté à mes yeux puisqu'il a deux ans de plus que moi n'est ni à avaler, ni à recracher, seulement à connaître, les yeux fermés je vois sa langue comme la langue de bœuf à table, ma langue reconnaît tout de suite la forme que j'ai jusqu'alors seulement vu avec mes yeux, dans la glace ou dans l'assiette, maintenant ma langue voit la langue de l'autre, et la mienne par reflet, on n'est pas à table, le goût de la langue cuite arrive, ce goût que j'endure pour être au goût de mes parents ogres, pour gagner un point sur mon frère qui n'a pas la force, cette nuit comme lui je faillis, elle entre dans ma bouche, elle ressort, c'est ma nouvelle vie qui ne s'avale pas, elle me laisse de la salive, ce n'est pas dégoûtant, c'est une langue étrangère.

after a party i do it, with my childhood friend annette, i know i have to open my mouth to begin to cease to be a child, a boy at least two years older, with red hair, whom i've never seen before this party, we're part of a foursome, he's with a friend, i'm with a friend, we're on a grassy knoll in a neighborhood of a small town in west germany, ludwigshafen, or tübingen, i think it's tübingen, because my friend lived there and i'm with her, and ludwigshafen is where she lived before, after moving away from the street where we had become friends, in freiburg, i don't remember well though it's quite simple, when i close my eyes the boy puts his tongue in my mouth, i don't know what to do, yes, thanks to having studied the ten variations of the tongue kiss i know that it will come into my mouth, that at the approach of his tongue i can do some things with mine, but i can also just open my mouth like i learned to do playing mund auf augen zu and see what happens, open your mouth and close your eyes and in your mouth you'll get a surprise, tastes, forms, something i have not seen and that i have to get to know with the eyes of my tongue, i can let it reach to the back of my throat, to where i can never see my tongue, unless this is a trick and i have to spit it out, you never know with this game, the tongue of this red haired boy, in my eyes much more experienced because he is a couple of years older than me, is neither to be swallowed nor spat out, just to be known, with eyes closed, his tongue appears like the beef tongue on the table, my tongue immediately recognizes the form that till now i've only seen with my eyes, in the mirror or the plate, now my tongue sees the tongue of the other, and my own by reflection, we're not at the table, the taste of the cooked tongue comes back, the taste i endure to please my ogre parents, to gain a point over my brother who hasn't the strength, this evening, like him, i fail, it enters my mouth, gets out again, it's my new life that's not to be swallowed, it leaves me some saliva, it's not disgusting, it's a foreign tongue.

un petit tas plus loin je suis un tas de chair et de dents chauds. mais au moins je reste chez moi le matin. ça n'a rien à voir avec le passé. le passé étant passé n'est plus à voir et à revoir. je passe en vélo sur le pont avant la porte d'aubervilliers, ce sont les voies des chemins de fer de l'est qu'on traverse, il y a un centre d'enregistrement pour les étrangers et certains y campent pour avoir une place le lendemain. je ne m'arrête pas mais j'ai envie. je pédale. je ne sais plus comment je voulais passer au passé à partir, si, je ne suis pas née étrangère, mais je le suis devenue volontiers. je ne fais plus la queue pour arriver devant une blonde désagréable qui me dit vos papiers vos papiers, ce n'est pas en règle. j'ai une carte de séjour sur laquelle il y a marqué : titre illimité. j'en ai même deux, car la première perdue m'est revenue une fois remplacée. j'ai le titre illimité original et j'ai le titre illimité duplicata. je n'ai pas le droit de voter où je vis mais j'y suis doublement illimitée.

quand je suis étrangère la première fois, sur l'île de manhattan, j'ai le droit de planter des clous dans le parquet parce que l'appartement est un taudis aux yeux de ma mère. je bricole doucement, c'est une terre, je fais un enclos avec des drapeaux jouets qu'on a eu sur le bateau, des tiges en bois fins, comme trois fois un cure dent. je suis seule dans la pièce, je ne sais pas ce que font mes frères. ils sont sûrement deux dans la chambre. après on n'a pas eu de chambre, mais l'appartement était plus habitable pour ma mère.

a little bit further on i'm a heap of flesh and warm teeth. but at least i spend the morning at home. this has nothing to do with the past. the past being past is no longer to be considered or reconsidered. i bicycle across the bridge towards aubervillers, crossing the railroad tracks of the east, there's a foreigners' registration center and some are camped out to have a place in line the next morning, i don't stop though i'd like to, i pedal on, i no longer know how from the start i wanted to skip to the past, yes, i was not born a foreigner but i gladly became one. i don't get into line to reach an unpleasant blond woman who tells me your papers your papers, they're not in order. i have a visitor's document which says: permit unlimited. i even have two, as the first was lost and then returned. i have the original unlimited permit and the duplicate unlimited permit. where i live i don't have the right to vote but i'm doubly unlimited.

my first time as a foreigner, on the isle of manhattan, i have the right to drive some nails into the hardwood floor because in mother's eyes the apartment is so shabby. i putter around, it's a land, i make an enclosure out of the toy flags we got on the ship, some thin wooden rods three times the width of a tooth pick. i'm alone in the room, i don't know what my brothers are doing. surely they are both in the bedroom. later we didn't get bed-rooms, but the apartment was more habitable for my mother.

de but en blanc, sans les lits, avec les nouvelles taches sur les mains, sans les faire, les lits, sans ouvrir la fenêtre, le dos encore dans la nuit, le soleil au-dessus des lunettes, je vois bien que je ne suis pas là dans un corps qui est le mien sauf par le pronom possessif et le départ, au départ c'est une cellule, mais depuis il ne doit plus y en avoir une seule comme là où je veux écrire, même à marburg quand je tourne autour de la barre de fer et que j'ai un trou dans la tête, ein loch im kopf, ces mots font mal aussi, et le sang le prouve, et qui le coud, je ne sais pas, pas mon père, et on dit après : gottseidank hat sie keine gehirnerschütterung, pas de tremblement du cerveau, et pourtant mon cerveau tremble. les vitres tremblent dans le rythme des moteurs de diesel ce matin. le présent se remet toujours devant ce que je veux me représenter, mes cheveux moins bouclés et coupés courts, assez courts pour qu'ils ne s'emmêlent pas, la même longueur que ma mère à peu près et je crois que c'est elle qui me les coupe.

mais depuis que je me souviens mieux, ma mère ne coupe jamais les cheveux, c'est moi qui coupe les siens. je me lève, je me réveille, je sors du lit. et alors ? sortons du lit. j'aimerais prendre quelqu'un dans mes bras. il faut aussi sortir de la maison pour ça, personne ne vient ici me déranger à écrire que personne n'est là, j'ai laissé partir les bras et les jambes et les torses et les têtes et les sexes et les pieds, en chaussures qui auraient pu m'empêcher d'écrire. il reste un animal, il dort, noir.

out of the blue, without the beds, with the new spots on the hands, without making them, the beds, without opening the window, the back still in the night, the sun above the eyeglasses, i see clearly that i'm not here in a body that is mine except for the possessive pronoun and the beginning, the beginning is a single cell, but later you shouldn't just have one like where i want to write, even in marburg when i turn around the iron rod, and i have a hole in my head, ein loch im kopf, also these words are painful, and the blood proves it, and who sews it back together, i don't know, not my father, and then they say: gottseidank hat sie keine gehirnerschütterung, no tremor of the brain, and yet my brain trembles. this morning the window panes tremble to the rhythm of the diesel motors. always the present appears in front of what i want myself to figure out, my hair less curly and cut short, short enough so it won't tangle, about the same length as my mother's and i think it's she who cuts it for me.

later when i remember more clearly, my mother never cuts my hair, i cut hers. i get up, i wake up, i get out of bed. and then? let's get out of bed. i wish to hold someone in my arms. for that you have to leave the house. no one comes to disturb me as i write that no one is there, i've let go the arms, the legs, the torsos, the heads, sex parts, and the feet in shoes that could have kept me from writing. an animal remains, it sleeps, black.

JÉRÔME GAME

Flip-Book (Editions de l'Attente, 2007)

À Los Angeles j'ai vu comment Ben Gazzara sort en *tux* à huit heures le matin le point aveugle après la nuit, s'encadre dans la porte. Les putes sont au repos. Les danseuses se rhabillent à six dans une voiture souple en cuir noir à la conduite souple. Une baleine démarre à l'embrayage souple, un grand chapeau garée devant la boîte de l'autre côté du Strip démarre doucement.

J'ai vu le sourire de Ben se tient droit backstage, ouvre la porte, se colle dans le cadre, sourit, sourit tout le temps, met une clope à sa bouche en coin, les yeux en coin. Ben sourit à son œillet rouge vif, son *tux*, son *bow*, son jabot est blanc, son mur est noir. Il reste là, la caméra est là, reste, il fait beau, le soleil étincelle déjà.

La caméra flotte sur le Strip devant la voiture face à Ben plein cadre. Le soleil rentre par la gauche en haut. La lumière liseré écharde le noir plein cadre. Il fait beau. Il attend. Il va aller tuer le bookmaker chinois ce soir, bleuté, plus tard.

*

JÉRÔME GAME

Flip-Book, translated by Barbara Beck

In Los Angeles I saw how Ben Gazzara goes out in a *tux* at eight in the morning blind spot after the night, appears framed in the doorway. The whores are off work. The dancers are putting their clothes back on six of them in a smooth car with black leather that drives smoothly. A whale starts up smooth geared, a land yacht parked in front of the club on the other side of the Strip starts up softly.

I saw Ben smiling standing straight backstage, opens the door, pushes into the frame, smiles, smiles the whole time, puts a cig into the corner of his mouth, eyes sideways. Ben smiles at his bright red carnation, his *tux*, his *bow*, his shirt front is white, his wall is black. He stays there, the camera is there, stays, it's a beautiful day, sun already sparkling.

The camera floats above the Strip in front of the car facing Ben full frame. Sunlight enters from upper left. The light's edge splinters black full frame. It's a beautiful day. He waits. He'll go kill the Chinese bookie in the evening, bluish, later on.

*

Je vois pas les nains de jardin, j'entends le bruit de la pelouse à ras de jardin. La voiture glisse, le break, dans Suburbia. L'arroseur tourne. J'vois pas arriver la musique, *Blue Velvet* me rentre dans la tête. La machine L.A. tourne à plein. J'vois pas L.A., j'vois Cinémascope en noir perlé les deux blondes.

On redescend la colline de West Hollywood. Les deux blondes, une brune, platines aux petits seins sont là. Je vois, je ne vois plus que ça. La nuit étoilée, la brune aux gros seins a les lèvres rouges, la coiffure immaculée, la raie sur le côté.

Le *driver,* son chauffeur, le garde du corps, éclairent la nuit à la portière. La lumière cuir crème foncée le plafonnier éclaire la route, les buissons. Il la fait remonter, elle démarre, il lui parle. Ça sent le chaud, la nuit est tiède, l'air est encore tout noir perlé des villas alentour. Elle a les ongles rouges.

Un verre coule un *drink* coule dans mon verre, un whisky gouleyant plan large coule dans mes yeux, mes bronches se réchauffent, un soufflet tiède les déplie. West Hollywood plan large glisse dans ma gorge.

Ben progresse en apnée souple sur les toits des villas de Bel Air, évite un chien, son smoking est complet, pénètre celle du bookmaker chinois. Les reflets bleus phosphorescents de la piscine éclairée dansent derrière lui, Ben dans l'entrefilet sans palmes et sans tuba nage dans l'image.

*

I don't see the garden gnomes, I'm hearing the sounds from the lawn at garden level. The car glides, the station wagon, in Suburbia. The sprinkler goes around. I don't see the music coming, *Blue Velvet* pops into my head. The L. A. machine is in full swing. I don't see L. A., I see Cinemascope in pearl black the two blondes.

We go back down the West Hollywood hill. The two blondes, one brunette, platinums with small breasts are there. I see it, I can see nothing else. The starry night, the brunette with big breasts has red lips, immaculate hairstyle, parted on the side.

The *driver*, his chauffeur, the bodyguard, light up the night from the car door. The light the leather dark cream colored the dome light shines on the road, the bushes. He makes her get back in, it starts up, he talks to her. You can smell the heat, the night is warm, the air still very pearl black of the houses nearby. She has red fingernails.

A glass pours a *drink* pours into my glass, a mellow whiskey wide shot pours into my eyes, my lungs heat up, a warm bellows unfolds them. West Hollywood wide shot slides down my throat.

Ben makes his way smoothly holding his breath across the roofs of houses in Bel Air, avoids a dog, his tuxedo is intact, enters the Chinese bookie's. Behind him flicker the phosphorescent blue reflections from the lit pool, Ben in the strip of light without flippers and without snorkel swims in the image.

*

Les grenouilles de la Légion font la brasse, les têtards. Ils avancent en crabe leur fusil mitrailleur en main, se déhanchent. Ils boîtent en kaki torse nu sous les barbelés dans le sable de haut en plongé. L'eau claire les fait voir, l'eau turquoise opaque, mi-profonde, où leur sang se disperse quand ils explosent contre une mine, quand les rotors du bateau.

Ils avancent dans le bleu en chaloupant, ils avancent calmement contre le rouge le jaune des affiches de la peinture des murs en ciment à Djibouti, képis beiges, en chantant. Ils portent l'un des leurs à bout d'épaule à l'aube.

Le caporal les fait danser torse nu dans le désert Santin disparaît. Le caporal explose dans les miroirs du dancing.

Les légionnaires creusent des trous au soleil couchant, pissent dans la nuit, se propulsent comment des têtards sous l'eau peu profonde près du banc de sable en progressant à travers tout l'écran liquide.

*

Gerry est perdu dans le désert dans le bleu de la nuit son ami est mort. Ne voit plus rien, ne peut plus avancer, ses jambes, son jean sont cristallisés par le sel.

Les deux taches noires Gerry et son ami avancent lentement dans le bleu noir. Sont ralenties. Irisent. Se figent. Sont soudain gerried.

La lumière aveugle Gerry voit une voiture noire au loin qui file sur le banc de sable. Son visage gercé rose repose sur l'appuie-tête crème en cuir.

*

The frogs of the Legion swim breaststroke, the tadpoles. They duck-walk with their automatic rifles in hand, wriggle their hips. They limp in khakis shirtless under barbed wire in the sand from above high angle shot. The clear water shows them, opaque turquoise water, semi-deep, where their blood disperses when they explode on a mine, when the boat's propellers.

They move forward swaying in the blue, they move forward calmly against the red the yellow of posters of painted cement walls in Djibouti, beige kepis, singing. They carry one of their own shoulder-high at dawn.

The corporal makes them dance shirtless in the desert Santin disappears. The corporal explodes in the dance hall mirrors.

The legionnaires dig holes at sunset, piss in the night, propel themselves like tadpoles under the shallow water near the sand bank making their way across the entire liquid screen.

*

Gerry is lost in the desert in the blue of night his friend is dead. Can't see anymore, can't move forward, his legs, his jeans crystallized with salt.

The two black spots Gerry and his friend move forward slowly in the black blue. Are slowed down. Become iridescent. Freeze. Are suddenly gerried.

The light blinds Gerry sees a black car in the distance speeding along over the sand bank. His face raw pink lies on the cream colored leather headrest.

*

Le bouton en cuivre de la porte part en flou dans l'appartement de Xavier, Catherine lisse les murs farinés amande pâle, elle détache son visage fatigué son désir, écrit avec son gros plume son carnet bourgeois bouge sa lèvre inférieure, elle attend.

La tache rouge mouillée la Porsche lisse doucement enchâssée au gris du bitume, l'*autostrada* l'échangeur anthracite se déploie. La caméra tilte d'un point à l'autre, équilibre gentiment la balance elle écoute le moteur.

Elle va vite, elle s'arrache, elle est belle, son bruit le plan reste vide quand elle est partie plein de l'échangeur vide sans elle, elle est loin. Le goudron mazouteux anthracite tient l'image, le ciel est bas.

Le bruit s'arrache les lumières clignotent. Le plat du cadre est creusé, le plat de la forêt noire à deux fois trois voies est mouillé ça gicle, à la surface.

La ligne bleue électrique horizontale, la station service de nuit dans le vert foncé marron de la forêt noire le rouge de la tache s'arrête au milieu, longe les lignes grises de ciment liseré blanc de l'*autobahn*, la peau de porcelaine les arcades sourcilières de Catherine les arêtes de son nez les yeux baissés sont à Paris.

*

The copper doorknob fades into a blur in Xavier's apartment, Catherine smooths the powdery pale almond walls, she turns away her tired face her desire, writes with her big fountain pen her bourgeois notebook moves her lower lip, she waits.

The wet red spot the Porsche presses down smooth into the gray asphalt, the *autostrada* the dark gray cloverleaf unfolds. The camera tilts from one point to another, gently balancing the scales it listens to the engine.

It's going fast, it tears past, it's beautiful, the sound the scene remains empty after it's gone full of the cloverleaf empty without it, it's already far. The oily dark gray tarmac holds the image, the sky is low.

The sound tears past lights flicker. The flat of the frame is hollowed out, the flat of the black forest twice three lanes is wet splattered, on the surface.

Horizontal electric blue line, the gas station at night in the dark green brown of the black forest the red spot comes to a stop in the middle, moves along the gray lines of cement white-edged of the *autobahn*, the porcelain skin the arch of Catherine's eyebrows the bridge of her nose the lowered eyes are in Paris.

*

La caméra recule ellipse de la salle de bain blanc cassé lumière à l'encadrement de la chambre marron foncé. Il se lisse les cheveux gomina, sa peau glabre abricot ses épaules lisses découpent le maillot de corps blanc vif ses cheveux noirs au lit, à la chambre minuscule, lit défait en robe fourreau en pointu négligé sa choucroute noire remonte, effilée, mince, de longs bras taille de guêpe elle proteste, véhémente, allongée, assise, récrimine. La caméra danse immobile entre les murs bleus, il pleut, la fenêtre sur le noir de Hong Kong il encaisse sobrement il sourit. Elle aussi.

Ses yeux sont mats ses narines épatées son regard mélancolique sa moustache est collée.

Ils jouent à *cats and dogs*. Ils jouent à *il existe un oiseau sans pattes qui dort dans le vent et se pose seulement le jour de sa mort*. Ils jouent à *il pleut doucement dans les flaques dehors*.

Avec par ordre d'apparition à l'écran :
The Killing of a Chinese Bookie (John Cassavetes, 1976), *Blue Velvet* (David Lynch, 1986), *Beau travail* (Claire Denis, 1999), *Gerry* (Gus Van Sant, 2002), *Le Vent de la nuit* (Philippe Garrel, 1999), *Days of Being Wild* (Wong Kar Wai, 1991).

The camera backs up ellipsis from the bathroom off white light to the doorway of the dark brown bedroom. He smooths down his brilliantined hair, his hairless skin apricot-colored his smooth shoulders stand out in the bright white singlet his black hair on the bed, to the tiny bedroom, rumpled bed in a sheath dress in a pointy negligee her black beehive moves up again, tapered, slender, long arms wasp waist she protests, vehement, lying down, sitting, recriminates. The camera dances immobile between the blue walls, it's raining, the window on Hong Kong blackness he bears it soberly he smiles. So does she.

His eyes are dull his nostrils flat his gaze melancholy his moustache sticks.

They're playing at *cats and dogs*. They're playing at *there exists a bird without feet that sleeps in the wind and only alights on the day of its death*. They're playing at *it's raining softly into the puddles outside*.

In order of appearance:
The Killing of a Chinese Bookie (John Cassavetes, 1976), *Blue Velvet* (David Lynch, 1986), *Beau travail* (Claire Denis, 1999), *Gerry* (Gus Van Sant, 2002), *Le Vent de la nuit* (Philippe Garrel, 1999), *Days of Being Wild* (Wong Kar Wai, 1991).

CHRISTOPHE TARKOS

extracts from *Ecrits poétiques* (Paris: P.O.L, 2008)

CHANSON 1

Je suis content
Je vais à l'usine
Aujourd'hui Je vis
Je vais travailler aujourd'hui
Je suis sur le chemin matin
Je vais à l'usine C'est je c'est je
Je suis content
Je vais à l'usine
Aujourd'hui Je vis
Je vais travailler aujourd'hui
Je suis sur le chemin matin
Je vais à l'usine C'est je c'est je
Je ne vais pas pas à l'usine
Je ne vais pas pas travailler
Je ne suis pas pas de travail
aujourd'hui je vais à l'usine
Je chemin
Je matin
Je vais Je sais Je suis heureux
Matin aujourd'hui
Je ne vais pas pas à l'usine
aujourd'hui Je suis le chemin
allant travailler à l'usine
ce matin
Je ne suis pas ne pas aller
usiner ce jour

CHRISTOPHE TARKOS

extracts from *Ecrits poétiques*, translated by Jérôme Game
(revised version of texts published in *Quid*, no. 3 (1999))

SONG 1

I am happy
I am going to the factory
Today I live
I am going to work today
I am on the way morning
I am going to the factory It's I it's I
I am happy
I am going to the factory
Today I live
I am going to work today
I am on the way morning
I am going to the factory It's I it's I
I am not not going to the factory
I am not not going to work
I am not not on the job
today I'm going to the factory
I way
I morning
I go I know I'm happy
Morning today
I'm not not going to the factory
today I am the way
going to work in the factory
this morning
I am not not going
manufacturing this day

Je ne vais pas pas aller à l'usine
Je ne suis pas pas chemin
Je ne suis pas pas matin
Je ne suis pas pas travailler
Je suis content d'aller à l'usine
C'est matin aujourd'hui
Je suis chemin
Je vais travailler
Je suis content
Aujourd'hui ma vie
chemin de matin
Je suis content
Je marche aller travailler
vers l'usine
aujourd'hui c'est la vie

*

I'm not going not to go to the factory
I'm not no way
I'm not no morning
I'm not no working
I'm happy to go to the factory
It's morning today
I'm way
I'm going to work
I'm happy
Today my life
morning way
I'm happy
I walk going to work
towards the factory
today it's life

*

CHANSON 4

Révolution
Je cherche un camarade
pour faire la Révolution
En avant
Nous prendrons les faits,
nous irons avec les Faits
Faire la révolution
Devant la grande Substance
Le monde s'éveillera
On étendra la révolution
à la grande Substance
Il n'y a pas que les Doigts dans
la Main
O tro lo lo Ie to tro lo lo
Le Sac grandiose la Révolution
Incommensurable
Min min lon lon fan fan don
don ma Dondé
On répandra écraser
écrase croustille, écrase agrandit
écrase étend, écrase multiplie
écrase étoile, écrase disparaît
Ou On l'Ecrase ou on le Tire
Ou il Gonfle
L'écraser et le manger
et le gonfler et le tirer
et le parler et le croustiller
et l'étoiler et l'être et l'enculer
L'être et l'enculer
C'est la révolution

*

SONG 4

Revolution
I'm looking for a comrade
to make the Revolution
Onwards
We'll take the facts
we shall go with the Facts
Make the revolution
Before the great Substance
The world shall awake
We'll spread the revolution
to the great Substance
There's not only Fingers in
the Hand
O tro lo lo Ie to tro lo lo
The grand Sacking the Revolution
Incommensurable
Min min lon lon fan fan don
don my Dondy
We'll spread crushing
crush crisps, crush expands
crush extends, crush multiplies
crush fans out, crush disappears
Either We Crush it or we Pull it
or it Swells
To crush it and eat it
and inflate it and drag it
and speak it and crisp it
and fan it out and be it and bugger it
To be it and bugger it
It's the revolution

*

1

Je t'aime. Je t'aime toi. J'ai besoin de toi. J'aime ce qui existe. Je t'aime toi. Tu es là. J'aime ce qui existe plus que ce qui n'existe pas. Je m'enfonce. Tu es vivante. Je t'aime. J'ai besoin de qui vit. J'aime d'amour. Je ne sais plus ce que tu es. Je m'enfonce. J'ai le vertige. Je t'aime. C'est toi que j'aime. Tu es. J'aime ce qui est. J'ai besoin de ce qui est. Je t'aime. C'est toi que j'aime, toi plus que tout autre, toi plus que tout ce qui existe. Je suis amoureux de toi. Je t'aime plus que tout ce qui n'est pas toi. Toi, tu es là. Je tombe dans tes bras, je veux te prendre dans mes bras. Je suis pris de vertige, tu existes. Je n'aimerai rien de tout ce qui n'existe pas que toi, que toi, tu es. J'aime ce qui est plus que tout ce qui n'est pas, je m'enfonce, c'est toi que j'aime.

*

3

Tu es belle. Je vais t'aimer d'un amour amoureux. Je t'entends. Je vais t'aimer. Tu es si belle. Je sais que je ne résisterai pas à ta beauté. Je vais descendre, je vais t'entendre, je ne peux pas résister, je vais plonger. Je m'apporterai. Tu es si belle, si jeune, si vive, si évanouissante, je me perds. Je vais être à toi. Je t'entends, je suis déjà vers toi, je descends, je ne supporte pas, je plonge. Ta beauté m'attire. Je suis attiré, tu es si belle, je vais t'aimer. À la beauté de ta licence, je coule vers toi sans résistance, c'est à toi que je suis, je t'aime, je me porte à toi, tu es une déesse, je suis voyant ta beauté pris, ne voyant que toi, je suis à toi, tu es belle, je me porte, je ne résiste pas, je descends.

*

LOVE

1

I love you. You I love you. I need you. I love what exists. You I love you. You're here. I love what exists more than what doesn't exist. I'm sinking in. You're alive. I love you. I need who's alive. I love out of love. I no longer know what you are. I'm sinking in. I'm dizzy. I love you. It's you whom I love. You are. I love what is. I need what is. I love you. It's you whom I love, you more than any other, you more than any thing else that exists. I am in love with you. I love you more than any thing that is not you. You, you're here. I fall in your arms, I want to take you in my arms. I feel dizzy, you exist. I shall love nothing of what doesn't exist but you, you only, you are. I love what is more than any thing that isn't, I'm sinking in, it is you whom I love.

*

3

You're beautiful. I am going to love you of a love in love. I can hear you. I'm going to love you. You are so beautiful. I know I won't resist your beauty. I will go down, I will hear you, I can't resist, I will dive. I will bring myself. You are so beautiful, so young, so lively, so vanishing, I lose myself. I will be yours. I can hear you, I'm already towards you, I'm going down, I can't bear, I dive. Your beauty attracts me. I'm drawn to, you're so beautiful, I'm going to love you. At the beauty of your license, I sink towards you unresisting, you I belong to, I love you, I transport myself to you, you're a goddess, I am seeing your beauty caught, seeing only you, I'm yours, you're beautiful, I transport myself, I do not resist, I'm going down.

*

5

Je t'embrasse. Je prends ta bouche avec ma bouche, tu prends ma bouche avec ta bouche, elles se touchent. J'ouvre tes lèvres avec ma bouche, tu ouvres mes lèvres à tes lèvres, à ta bouche, à ta langue, tu tournes sa langue dans sa bouche, je tourne ta langue dans ma bouche, je découvre ta bouche, tu découvres la sensation de ma bouche, ma langue douce, avec ta langue, j'enveloppe ta langue dans ma langue, je la mélange, tu tournes ta langue, tu la mélanges, elles se touchent, ils se mélangent, je caresse ta langue , je t'aime, tu me laisses entrer, je laisse glisser ma langue, elles s'aiment, ta langue est dans ma bouche, tu caresses ma langue, tu m'aimes.

*

9

Je ne t'aime pas mais je t'aimais, je ne t'aime pas, pourtant je t'aimais beaucoup, tu ne t'aimes pas, tu m'aimais beaucoup, je ne t'aime pas, pourtant, tout mon amour était pour toi, tant je t'aimais, à ce moment-là, je t'aimais tant que, et toi tu m'aimais, nous nous aimions ensemble en vrai, j'aimais être tous les jours avec toi, être avec toi, j'ai aimé t'accompagner, te suivre, te voir, te respirer tous les jours, c'était avec un amour total que je t'aimais, j'étais en amour totalement avec toi, je ne t'aime pas, je ne t'aime pas, je ne t'aime pas, tu étais mon seul amour, je t'aimais de tout mon cœur, tu m'aimais et je t'aimais beaucoup.

5

I'm kissing you. I'm taking your mouth with my mouth, you're taking my mouth with your mouth, they touch. I open your lips with my mouth, you open my lips to your lips, to your mouth, to your tongue, you turn his tongue in his mouth, I turn your tongue in my mouth, I discover your mouth, you discover the sensation of my mouth, my soft tongue, with your tongue, I wrap your tongue up in my tongue, I mix it, you turn your tongue, you mix it, they touch, they mix, I caress your tongue, I love you, you let me in, I let my tongue slide, they love each other, your tongue is in my mouth, you caress my tongue, you love me.

*

9

I don't love you but I used to love you, I don't love you, yet I used to love you a lot, you don't love yourself, you used to love me a lot, I don't love you, yet, all my love was for you, so much I used to love you, at that time, I used to love you so much that, and you you used to love me, we used to love each other together for real, I used to love being with you every day, being with you, I've loved accompanying you, following you, seeing you, breathing you every day, it was out of a total love that I used to love you, I was in love totally with you, I don't love you, I don't love you, I don't love you, you were my only love, I used to love you with all my heart, you used to love me and I used to love you a lot.

OSCARINE BOSQUET

Mum is Down (Al Dante, 2012)

Où sommes nous quand tu passes

la tête dans la gazinière
par dessus la rambarde
la posologie de
l'accélérateur

contre le platane
dans la baie
le four
la cour

dans la cour le contour
de ton corps
chu

saut
vol
chute

ma
man?

*

OSCARINE BOSQUET

Mum is Down, translated by Simone Fattal and Cole Swensen
(Sausalito, California: The Post-Apollo Press, 2014)

Where are we when you pass

head in the gas stove
leaning over the window rail
the dosage
of the accelerator

against the plane tree
in the bay
the oven
the courtyard

in the courtyard the outline
of your body
fallen

leap
flight
fall

mom
me

*

Est-ce toi maman le loup qui invente ?
Et la marâtre qui ne serait pas toi ?
Quand la mère ne veut plus de l'enfant la marâtre
envoie la petite fille dans la forêt
miroir, miroir dis-moi qui
qui est la plus belle
même si le chasseur fit manger à la reine un cœur de biche
la jeune fille ne vivra qu'avec sept nains d'hommes
à moins de croire au baiser du prince qui délie
la fille des mots de la mère.

Mommy are you the crafty wolf?
or are you the stepmother?
When the mother no longer wants the child
the stepmother sends her into the forest
mirror, mirror tell me who
who is the fairest
when the hunter makes the queen eat the heart of the doe
the young girl will only live with seven dwarves
does she believe in the prince's kiss which untangles
her from her mother's words.

OSCARINE BOSQUET

participe présent (Le bleu du ciel, 2009)

[from ROSA LUXEMBOURG]

Rosa voudrait que je cesse de m'apitoyer sur le monde
au lieu d'y croire mon ton pleurard
gémissements et soupirs
croire au monde
malgré toutes les horreurs de la guerre
je ne me souviens pas de tous les endroits
où je suis en guerre Rosa voudrait
que je cesse de soutenir les pleutres
les lâches et les agents de la terreur
les grenouilles des marais.

–Il y a le choix entre l'action
et l'inaction l'action donne
la force organise
ce que nous ne pourrions imaginer

tout s'apprend y compris ne pas déguerpir.

*

OSCARINE BOSQUET

present participle, translated by Sarah Riggs and Ellen LeBlond-Schrader
(Iowa City & Paris: La Presse, 2013)

[from **ROSA LUXEMBOURG**]

Rosa wanted me to stop commiserating with the world
instead of believing my cowering
sighs and groans
to believe in the world
despite all the war horrors
I don't remember all the places
where I am at war Rosa would like
me to stop supporting the cowards
the slackers and agents of terror
the swamp frogs

– There's the choice between action
and inaction action gives
strength organizes
what we couldn't imagine

everything can be learned including not to leave.

*

[from PRÉSENT CONTINU]

Je ne me souviens pas où est la Tchétchénie
sur les cartes c'est en bas à cause de la Russie qui est en haut
à l'est la Caspienne d'où vient le pétrole sur la carte coule
dans la plaine au beau milieu en plein cœur
une ligne de pétrole Bakou-Novorossisk
avec des robinets clandestins tout le long
alimentent le trafic de tous les combattants
mais le boucher dans sa tenue de plombier
ferme les robinets ouvre une route par le Daghestan.

Nous sommes entrés en Tchétchénie pourchasser les terroristes
c'était pendant l'hiver au début de septembre
c'était Alkhma-kala
l'ordre était de poursuivre les terroristes jusque
de les étrangler jusque
la canaille les terroristes
sont des hommes entre 25 et 40 ans
au visage fraîchement rasé
c'etait pendant l'hiver au début de janvier dans le village de Daï
c'était pendant l'hiver dans le village de Nokhtchi-Keloï
c'était le 11 janvier 2002 dans le district de Chatoï
l'ordre était que
l'ordre était de
jusque.

[from PRESENT CONTINUOUS]

I cannot remember where Chechnya is
on the map it's below because Russia is on top
the Caspian sea to the east where oil comes from
runs on the map on the plain in the very center
in the very heart the Baku-Novorossiysk pipeline
with clandestine faucets all along
feeds the traffic of all the fighters
but the butcher in plumber's clothes
turns off the faucet opens a road through Dagestan.

We have come to Chechnya to hunt down the terrorists
it was already winter in early September
it was at Alkhan-Kala
the order was to pursue the terrorists all the way
strangle them all the way
the scoundrel the terrorists
are men between 25 and 40
with freshly shaven faces
it was winter in early January in the village of Dai
it was winter in the village of Nokhchi-Keloi
it was the 11th of January 2002 in the district of Chatoi
the order was to
the order was then
all the way.

ANNE-JAMES CHATON

Vies d'hommes illustres d'après les écrits d'hommes illustres (Al Dante, 2011)

VIE DE... *

d'après Giambattista Vico

Mon 1er tomba la tête la première du haut d'une échelle.
Mon 2e eut la partie droite du crâne fracassée.
Mon 3e faillit rester idiot.
Mon 4e est d'un naturel mélancolique et pénétrant.
Mon 5e fréquenta l'école de grammaire.
Mon 6e étudia la logique.
Mon 7e eut pour maître un bon summuliste.
Mon 8e erra hors du droit chemin d'une jeunesse bien réglée.
Mon 9e s'enferma chez lui une année entière.
Mon 10e acquit une copie de Vultejus.
Mon 11e lut les Institutions canoniques d'Henricus Canisius.
Mon 12e médita les sommes des lois.
Mon 13e tira avantage de la langue latine.
Mon 14e voulut pratiquer le barreau.
Mon 15e plaida en cour de Rote.
Mon 16e fut embrassé par Francesco Antonio Aquilante.
Mon 17e lu Regius.
Mon 18e fut menacé d'étisie.
Mon 19e se mit à étudier la langue toscane dans l'œuvre de ses princes.
Mon 20e sauta de la logique à la métaphysique.
Mon 21e étudia jusqu'à la cinquième proposition d'Euclide.
Mon 22e forma son ingegno aux heureux rapprochements.
Mon 23e passa neuf années dans la solitude.
Mon 24e composa une canzone sur le mariage du duc de Bavière avec la princesse Thérèse de Pologne.

ANNE-JAMES CHATON

Vies d'hommes illustres d'après les écrits d'hommes illustres,
translated by Nina Parish

LIFE OF...*

after Giambattista Vico

My 1st fell head first from the top of a ladder.
My 2nd had the right side of his cranium fractured.
My 3rd almost remained an idiot.
My 4th is of a melancholic and penetrating nature
My 5th went to grammar school.
My 6th studied logic.
My 7th had as a teacher a good summulist.
My 8th strayed from the straight and narrow of a well-adjusted youth.
My 9th shut himself away for a whole year.
My 10th acquired a copy of Vulteius.
My 11th read the Canonical Institutes of Henricus Canisius.
My 12th meditated on the surveys of laws.
My 13th cultivated the Latin language.
My 14th wanted to be called to the bar.
My 15th defended before the Rota.
My 16th received the congratulations of Francesco Antonio Aquilante.
My 17th read the Regius manuscript.
My 18th was in danger of phthisis.
My 19th turned to cultivation of the Tuscan tongue by study of its princes.
My 20th jumped from logic to metaphysics.
My 21st studied up to Euclid's fifth proposition.
My 22nd developed his ingegno for finding happy correspondences.
My 23rd spent nine years in solitude.
My 24th composed a canzone on the marriage of the Duke of Bavaria to Princess Theresa of Poland.

Mon 25e abandonna le grec étudié dans la seconde classe des Jésuites.
Mon 26e lut les auteurs latins sans le secours des notes.
Mon 27e n'était point de noble origine.
Mon 28e présenta sa candidature à une chaire de rhétorique qui ne rapportait pas plus de cent écus.
Mon 29e admirait Platon et Tacite.
Mon 30e découvrit un homme d'une sagesse vulgaire et absconse.
Mon 31e prouva que l'esprit humain est proportionnellement le Dieu de l'homme comme Dieu est l'esprit du Tout.
Mon 32e démontra que dans la République des Lettres il faut vivre en respectant la justice.
Mon 33e attaqua les faux savants qui font des études pour leur intérêt propre uniquement.
Mon 34e observa que l'homme en punition du péché est séparé de l'homme par la langue, par l'esprit et par le cœur.
Mon 35e publia une dissertation in-12 sur les presses de Felice Mosca.
Mon 36e traita amplement du secret des lois des anciens jurisconsultes romains.
Mon 37e chercha les principes de la sagesse plus loin que dans les fables des poètes.
Mon 38e fonda un système de médecine basé sur le chaud et le froid.
Mon 39e dégagea les points de Zénon des altérations qu'Aristote leur avait fait subir.
Mon 40e donna une définition du point comme ce qui n'a pas de parties.
Mon 41e posa comme principe de toutes les formes corporelles le coin.
Mon 42e écrivit une brochure sur la théorie médicale du lâche et du serré.
Mon 43e établit une étymologie universelle pour toutes les langues anciennes et modernes.
Mon 44e écrivit une canzone sur la rose.

My 25th gave up Greek studied in the second grade of the Jesuits.
My 26th read Latin authors without recourse to notes.
My 27th was definitely not of noble birth.
My 28th presented an application for a chair of rhetoric which did not yield more than 100 ducats.
My 29th admired Plato and Tacitus.
My 30th discovered a man of popular and recondite wisdom.
My 31st proved that the human mind is by analogy the god of man just as God is the mind of the whole of things.
My 32nd showed that in the Republic of Letters one must live in respect of justice.
My 33rd attacked the pseudo-scientists who carry out studies uniquely in their own interest.
My 34th observed that man under pain of sin is separated from man by tongue, mind and heart.
My 35th published a dissertation in duodecimo on the press of Felice Mosca.
My 36th amply treated the secret of the laws of ancient Roman jurisconsults.
My 37th looked for the principles of wisdom further back than in the fables of the poets.
My 38th founded a system of medicine based on heat and cold.
My 39th extricated Zeno's points from the distortions that Aristotle had made to them.
My 40th gave a definition of the point as that which has no parts.
My 41st posed the corner as the principle of all corporeal forms.
My 42nd wrote a brochure on medical theory of slack and tight.
My 43rd established a universal etymology of all languages living and dead.
My 44th wrote a canzone on the rose.

Mon 45e fut cruellement affecté de spasmes hypocondriaques dans le bras gauche.

Mon 46e fut le premier à publier un livre dans le goût de la typographie hollandaise.

Mon 47e déplut à quelques personnes en ramenant la philologie à des principes scientifiques.

Mon 48e lut les poèmes d'Homère à l'aide de quelques canons mythologiques qu'il s'était créé.

Mon 49e postula à la première chaire de droit du matin qui ne rapportait que six cent écus par an.

Mon 50e naquit pour la gloire de sa patrie, autrement dit l'Italie, puisque c'est là, et non au Maroc, qu'il est né.

Mon 51e découvrit un nouvel art critique.

Mon 52e découvrit la véritable origine des emblèmes héroïques qui fut un langage muet de toutes les premières nations.

Mon 53e donna l'idée d'une étymologie commune à toutes les langues originelles.

Mon 54e donna l'idée d'une autre étymologie des mots d'origine étrangère.

Mon 55e développa l'idée d'une étymologie universelle destinée à la science du langage.

Mon 56e prouva que la première époque et la première langue correspondent au temps des familles.

Mon 57e prouva que la seconde époque, dans laquelle se parlait la seconde langue, fut celle des premiers gouvernements civils.

Mon 58e prouva que la troisième époque, l'âge des hommes et des langues vulgaires, vient dans le temps des idées de la nature humaine entièrement développée.

Mon 59e fut professeur royal d'éloquence.

Mon 60e composa des inscriptions à l'occasion des funérailles de l'empereur Joseph.

My 45th was wracked by hypochondriac cramps in his left arm.

My 46th was the first to publish a book in the Dutch typographical style.

My 47th was disliked by some for bringing philology back to scientific principles.

My 48th read Homer's poem with help from some mythological canons that he had made for himself.

My 49th applied for the first morning chair of law which paid only six hundred ducats annually.

My 50th came into the world for the glory of his homeland, in other words, Italy, since it is there, and not in Morocco, that he was born.

My 51st discovered a new critical art.

My 52nd discovered the true origins of heroic insignia which were a dumb language of all the first nations.

My 53rd gave the idea of an etymology common to all original languages.

My 54th gave the idea of another etymology for words of foreign origin.

My 55th developed the idea of a universal etymology for the science of language.

My 56th proved that the first age and the first language coincide with the time of the families.

My 57th proved that the second age, in which the second language was spoken, was that of the first civil governments.

My 58th proved that the third age, the age of common men and vernacular languages, comes at the time of the ideas of a human nature completely developed.

My 59th was royal professor of eloquence.

My 60th composed inscriptions on the occasion of the funeral of Emperor Joseph.

Mon 61e composa des inscriptions à l'occasion des funérailles de l'impératrice Éléonore.

Mon 62e composa un épithalame à l'occasion du mariage de don Giambattista Filomarino avec donna Maria Vittoria Caracciolo.

Mon 63e composa une ode pindarique, mais en vers libre, dédiée à donna Marine Della Torre, duchesse de Carignan.

Mon 64e composa l'oraison funèbre d'Anna d'Aspromonte, comtesse d'Althan.

Mon 65e composa un discours pour la mort de donna Angiola Cimini, marquise della Petrella.

Mon 66e contracta un ulcère gangreneux à la gorge.

Mon 67e risqua la cure périlleuse des fumigations de cinabre.

Mon 68e subit une longue et grave maladie contractée pendant l'épidémie de catarrhe.

Mon 69e fut tourmenté par des douleurs convulsives dans les bras et les jambes.

Mon 70e fut en proie à un mal étrange qui lui dévora tout ce qu'il y a entre l'os inférieur de la tête et le palais.

Mon TOUT porte le nom d'une célèbre marque de chips*.

* Réponse Giambattista Vico

My 61st composed inscriptions on the occasion of the funeral of Empress Eleanor.

My 62nd composed an epithalamium on the occasion of the marriage of don Giambattista Filomarino to donna Maria Vittoria Caracciolo.

My 63rd composed a Pindaric ode, but in free verse, dedicated to donna Marina Della Torre, duchess of Carignano.

My 64th composed the funeral oration for Anna d'Aspermont, countess of Althann.

My 65th composed a speech on the death of donna Angiola Cimini, marchioness della Petrella.

My 66th contracted a gangrenous ulcer of the throat.

My 67th risked the dangerous remedy of cinnabar.

My 68th suffered a long and serious illness contracted during the epidemic of catarrh.

My 69th was tormented by convulsive pains in his arms and legs.

My 70th was prey to a strange disease that devoured all there is between the lower bone of the head and the palate.

My WHOLE rhymes with the name of the singer of *I'll Be Your Mirror**.

* Answer Giambattista Vico

JEAN-MARIE GLEIZE

Tarnac, un acte préparatoire (Paris: Seuil, 2011)

« la folie d'un ordre »

Le onze novembre à 5 heures la police traverse Toy-Viam avec des chiens.
Les cinq routes d'accès au village de Tarnac sont bloquées.
Le village est bouclé.
Un hélicoptère survole la zone.

150 policiers
60 de la *sdat* (sous-direction de l'antiterrorisme)
50 de la *dcri* (direction centrale du renseignement intérieur)
40 de la police judiciaire de Limoges

Les perquisitions commencent.
On ne trouve
ni armes, ni engins incendiaires, ni fers à béton, ni crochets métalliques.

Des étendues de fougères, des haies de fougères, des talus et des lits de fougères.

Un masque aux yeux fixes engloutit la tête d'un oiseau.

*

JEAN-MARIE GLEIZE

Tarnac, a preparatory act, ed. by Joshua Clover; translated by Joshua Clover, Abigail Lang and Bonnie Roy (Chicago: Kenning Editions, 2014)

"the folly of an order"

On eleven November at 5 a.m. the police cross Toy-Viam with dogs.
The five access roads to the village of Tarnac are blocked.
The village is sealed.
A helicopter surveys the zone.

150 policemen
60 from the *sdat* (sous-direction de l'antiterrorisme)
50 from the *dcri* (direction centrale du renseignement intérieur)
40 from the police judiciaire in Limoges

The house searches begin.
They find
neither weapons, nor explosives, nor incendiary bombs, nor steel reinforcement bars, nor metal hooks.

Stretches of ferns, hedges of ferns, banks and beds of ferns.

A mask with fixed eyes gulps down the head of a bird.

*

DOCUMENT « F », I [*la voie de pauvreté*]

« son apparence misérable disait assez où il plaçait son trésor »

« faites que le signe de notre communauté soit de ne jamais posséder rien en propre sous le soleil pour la gloire de votre nom, et de n'avoir d'autre bien que la mendicité »

« si nous possédions quelque chose il nous faudrait des armes pour nous défendre. De la possession naissent les difficultés et les disputes qui élèvent des obstacles à l'amour du prochain. C'est pourquoi nous ne voulons posséder aucune chose temporelle, aucune »

« si nous avions des biens il nous faudrait des armes et des lois pour les défendre. C'est pourquoi nous ne devons rien posséder, rien. »

« pour nous des cabanes de bois, aucun autre abri que les branches et des huttes, des cabanes. Il faut construire des cabanes »

*

DOCUMENT "F", I [the way of poverty]

"his miserable appearance clearly told where he put his treasure"

"let the sign of our community be to never possess anything of its own beneath the sun for the glory of your name, and to have no goods other than alms"

"if we possessed anything we would need weapons to defend ourselves. From ownership are born difficulties and disputes that pose obstacles to the love of the neighbor. This is why we do not want to possess any worldly thing, none"

"if we had goods we would need weapons and laws to protect them. This is why we should possess nothing, nothing at all."

"For us wood cabins, no shelter other than branches and huts, cabins. We must build cabins"

*

Alors, que devient l'image ? Elle se détache et tombe à la vitesse du vent. Ici, par temps d'orage le vent soulevait les charpentes et les brisait.

– Je fais tomber les voyelles.
– Il y en a deux, mais il n'y en a qu'une, c'est la première, la seule, la lettre noire, celle du commencement, dans l'eau de l'écluse ou du lavoir celle du milieu de l'image.

TRNC *est le nom filmé de ce village.* Il se construit d'un fragment fermé (ou jardin clos), cerné (ou « masse informe »).

Tu voulais photographier la nuit. Tu voyais le haut des arbres se détacher sur le ciel et c'était comme les dents d'une scie. Tu as tiré au hasard, lancé tes mains vers l'acier dur et froid qui coupait le ciel. Tu as pensé : « il n'y a plus rien entre Dieu et nous ».

C'est le sens de ces quatre photographies.

*

So what becomes of the image? It comes loose and falls with the wind's quickness. Here, in stormy weather the wind lifted and broke the house frames.

– I knock over the vowels.
– There are two of them, but there is only one, the first one, the only, the black letter, that of beginning, in the water of the sluice or the washhouse, that of the image's center.

TRNC *is the filmed name of this village*. It's built from a sealed fragment (or closed garden), surrounded (or "formless mass").

You wanted to photograph the night. You saw the tree-tops in relief against the sky like saw teeth. You shot at random, threw up your hands toward the hard and cold steel which cut the sky. You thought: "there is nothing between God and us."

That's the sense of these four photographs.

*

- je reprends à partir du mot « communiste »

Communiste est ce mot enfermé dans l'eau, ce corps enfermé dans l'eau.
Ici à Tarnac le brouillard se couche à la surface de l'eau
froisse les talus de fougères c'est la nuit.

Aucune revendication aucun message, *la politique comme négation de la politique*
la descente à la rivière
la chute de la photographie sur le goudron
la lumière de froid et d'incendie, les pentes, les pentes
le chemin de Javaud, le chemin de Larpée
l'écriture déviée cassée comme ça, comme la voix
comme elle
comme sans réponse.

Il faut (il faut construire des cabanes)
Il faut

Je connais un arbre
Il faut construire des cabanes dans les arbres
se faire un lit de fougères
bloquer gares périphériques autoroutes usines
supermarchés aéroports,
utiliser les accidents du sol

- I pick up from the word "communist."

Communist is this word caught in water, this body caught in water.
Here in Tarnac the fog sits on the surface of the water
creases the banks of ferns it's night.

No claim of responsibility no message, *politics as*
the negation of politics
the way down to the river
the photograph falling on the tar
the light of cold and conflagration, the slopes, the slopes
the Javaud path, the Larpée path
the writing deviated broken like that, like the voice
like it
like no response.

One must (one must build cabins)
One must

I know a tree
One must build cabins in the trees
make oneself a bed of ferns
block stations ring roads highways factories
supermarkets airports,
use the accidents of the ground

BÉATRICE BONHOMME

Variations du visage et de la rose (Jégun: L'arrière-pays, 2013)

VISAGE DU FAYOUM

Quand on entre dans la maison la présence du visage emplit l'ombre et c'est comme une clarté translucide qui se déposerait sur un cercueil peint. Le portrait est là pour ne pas tomber dans l'oubli. Le visage n'est plus peint sur la tombe. La maison comme un sépulcre a gardé le visage en elle. On ouvre la maison tel le secret d'une pyramide et le visage apparaît dans la lumière. On remarque surtout la présence du regard qui vous suit partout dans la pièce.

1

Ce visage comme le portrait le plus ancien découvert dans le Fayoum. Posé sur le sarcophage en masque funéraire, réalisé dans du bois de tilleul ou de sycomore. Collé sur le lin.

Il n'y a pas de vacances à l'amour. Cette fresque d'un visage a envahi l'espace de la maison. La demeure s'est blottie autour d'une rose rouge qui demeure le cœur de l'enfance.

La rose est rouge comme la terre lorsqu'elle soulève ses poussières de verre dans l'été brûlant. Ce n'est pas le cristal sous les pieds qui crisse mais juste cette poussière de verre d'une terre à quartz, là où ne reste aucune empreinte, même pas celle en trèfle d'un chat qui passe en dansant.

2

Le peintre, en plus de l'or, n'a utilisé que quatre couleurs : le noir, le rouge et deux sortes d'ocre.

Sur la toile de lin, sur la toile de jute accrochée au mur, le visage est posé. Le visage possède une terrible présence.

BÉATRICE BONHOMME

Variations du visage et de la rose, translated by Michael Bishop

THE FACE OF FAIYUM

When one enters the house the presence of the face fills the shadows and it is as though a translucid brilliance were coming to settle upon a painted coffin. The portrait is there to avoid falling into oblivion. The face is no longer painted onto the tomb. The house like a sepulchre has kept the face within itself. One unlocks the house like the secret of a pyramid and the face appears in the light. What is above all noticeable is the presence of the gaze following you everywhere in the room.

1

The face, the most ancient portrait discovered in Faiyum. Placed upon the sarcophagus and a funeral mask, made from linden or sycamore wood. Glued onto linen.

There are no holidays from love. This fresco of a face has invaded the house's space. The dwelling place has settled about a red rose that is still the heart of childhood.

The rose is red like earth when it bears up its glassy dust in the burning summer. It is not the crystal underfoot that crunches but just this glassy dust of a quartz earth, upon which no footprint remains, not even the clover-like one of a cat dancing by.

2

The painter, in addition to gold, has used only four colours: black, red, and two kinds of ochre.

Upon the linen canvas, the jute canvas, hanging on the wall, the face is placed. The face possesses a terrible presence.

Le portrait est peint sur bois (de tilleul) ou sur lin. Des couleurs ont été mélangées à de la cire d'abeille.

On peut suivre encore aujourd'hui les traces de pinceau du peintre ou les marques de la lame dont il s'est servi pour étaler la couleur.

3

La rose est la solitude d'un cœur, un cœur seul au cœur de l'hiver, nul ne pensant plus à lui et ne venant le visiter. La rose est le cœur de la vie restée figée dans l'hiver, dans le tableau d'un visage qui ne commande plus qu'aux ombres.

C'est le calme de la mort qui a empli la maison rouge, laissant le givre se prendre et enserrer la patte du chat qui voulait saisir le vent.

Le chat marche sur la page avec la fleur de ses pattes et il reste enserré dans la page comme une fleur de gris sur du blanc.

La maison n'est plus habitée, le cœur n'est plus habité, la vie a déserté ce lieu. La patte du chat est restée enfermée dans le blanc de la page, comme le piège se referme sur la sveltesse de sa course. Il reste peu d'énergie désormais dans ce corps de petit félin, prisonnier de l'emprise des mots.

4

La chair de ces pigments fait pourtant penser au pain de la vie. Le visage fait lever la vie.

Les portraits peints sur des sarcophages ont été découverts dans un pays fertile qu'on nommait le jardin d'Egypte.

The portrait is painted onto wood (linden) or linen. Colours have been mixed in with beeswax.

Still today one can follow the painter's brush tracings or the markings of the blade he used to spread colour evenly.

3

The rose is the solitude of a heart, a heart alone in the heart of winter, no one thinking of it any longer or coming to visit it. The rose is the heart of life that has become stuck in winter, in the picture of a face that now holds sway over mere shadows.

It is the calmness of death that has filled the red house, leaving the frost to set in and grip the paw of the cat that wanted to grasp the wind.

The cat walks across the page with the flower of its paws and remains in the tight grip of the page like a flower of greyness on white.

The house is no longer lived in, the heart is lived in no more, life has deserted the place. The cat's paw remains still in the grip of the page's whiteness, as the trap locks tight about the svelte grace of its swiftness. Henceforth little energy dwells in this small feline body, prisoner of the ascendancy of words.

4

The flesh of the pigments yet makes one think of the bread of life. The face leavens life.

The portraits painted on sarcophagi were discovered in a fertile land people used to call the garden of Egypt.

Les portraits peints à l'usage des morts entreprenant en compagnie d'Anubis, le dieu à tête de Chacal, leur voyage vers le royaume d'Osiris.

Les personnages représentés sont vivants et viennent de s'avancer timidement à notre rencontre.

5

Le regard nous parle à chacun en particulier.

Ce qui se produit lorsqu'on se trouve face aux visages du Fayoum.

Des images d'hommes et de femmes qui ne lancent aucun appel, ne demandent rien mais déclarent qu'ils sont en vie et que toute personne qui les regarde l'est aussi.

Ce qui se passe devant le visage du tableau.

Le visage confirme que la vie était et demeure un don.

6

Cette fresque d'un visage a pris la place d'une enfance.

Les enfants courent comme des indiens dans la fresque.

Les enfants entrent dans le bas-relief et exhibent des boucliers de couleur.

Les enfants se prennent dans la farine et s'engluent dans le pigment de la fresque.

Ils meurent étouffés, écrasés sur la palette, et ne laissent que des taches de couleurs sur le blanc neigeux de la fresque.

The portraits painted for the use of the dead undertaking, in the company of Anubis, the jackal-headed god, their journey towards the kingdom of Osiris.

The individuals represented are alive and have just begun their timid advance towards us.

5

Their gaze speaks to each one of us.

This is what happens when one finds oneself before the faces of Faiyum.

Images of men and women who do not call out, ask for nothing, but declare they are alive and that each person gazing upon them is alive too.

This is what comes to pass before the picture's face.

The face confirms that life was and remains ever a gift.

6

The fresco of a face has taken up the place of childhood.

The children are running like Indians in the fresco.

The children enter the bas-relief and present shields of colour.

The children are caught up in the flour and become stuck in the fresco's pigment.

They die, suffocating, crushed upon the palette, and all that is left of them are patches of colour upon the snowy whiteness of the fresco.

7

Les enfants ont donné des couleurs au visage.

Ils ont fardé le visage des couleurs de la vie avec le sang de la rose rouge.

Les enfants sont épinglés dans la fresque comme des papillons morts aux ailes colorées.

La rose est posée sanglante sur la table, face au tableau d'un visage. Elle rend hommage à la vie qui demeure dans le visage. Le visage qui s'était éteint sur la plaque de marbre a repris des couleurs dans le tableau.

8

La vie désormais s'est transportée dans le tableau et l'homme, exsangue, a posé la rose sur ses joues.

Les visages plus précieux encore, ils le sont, parce que le regard peint est tout entier concentré sur cette vie qu'il sait qu'il va perdre un jour.

Le visage nous regarde, son regard nous suit partout dans la pièce éclairée de rayons, il regarde comme un non-disparu.

9

Les petits chevaux de Tarquinia ont emmêlé leurs pattes au filet et sont restés incrustés dans le sable.

Il n'est demeuré que ce plongeur de Paestum pour cueillir ce qu'il restait des rires et des joies du voyage.

Le plongeur a pénétré dans la fresque, il est entré en eaux profondes pour retrouver les eaux libres de l'amour.

7

The children have given colour to the face.

They have made up the face of the colours of life with the blood of the red rose.

The children are pinned to the fresco like dead butterflies with their coloured wings.

The rose is placed bleeding upon the table, before the painting of a face. It pays homage to the life dwelling in the face. The face that had passed away upon the marble slab has found a new freshness in the picture.

8

Life henceforth has shifted into the picture and the man, bloodless, has placed the rose upon his cheeks.

The still more precious faces are so because the painted gaze is entirely concentrated upon the life it knows it will one day lose.

The face looks out upon us, its gaze follows us everywhere about the room illuminated with rays of light, the gaze of one who has not left us.

9

The little horses of Tarquinia have tangled up their hooves in the net and now remain embedded in the sand.

Only the diver from Paestum has stayed behind to gather up what was left of the laughter and the joys of the journey.

The diver has penetrated the fresco. He has moved into deep waters to recover the free waters of love.

10

Le portrait est posé directement sur le visage du mort.

Le visage est peint avec une expression de vie saisissante.

Le visage a été peint pour ne pas tomber dans l'oubli.

Mais pourquoi le nageur est-il figé sur la toile devant des enfants qui passent et repassent en riant ?

Les enfants ont quitté le musée et ils sont devenus des mots. Ils ont écrit le mot visage dans la lumière. Tout près de ce mot a poussé une rose.

10

The portrait is placed directly onto the face of the dead man.

The face is painted with a stunning expression of livingness.

The face has been painted so as to not fall into oblivion.

But why is the swimmer stuck motionless on the canvas in front of children going to and fro amidst their laughter?

The children have left the museum and have become words. They have written the word face in the light. Right by this word a rose has sprung forth.

STÉPHANE BOUQUET

Les amours suivants (Seyssel: Champ Vallon, 2013)

[From « Les Amours »]

II

Dans le métro je lève la tête du livre et
oh… il tient des fleurs pas pour moi
et une boîte à gâteaux
pas pour moi… une fois de plus où un visage est un dangereux
débarquement d'espérance
par ex. nous ne sommes pas déserts de demains… la preuve tu es
là… débutant à la lisière
des actes humains et ta peur de revenir
sans sourires… ça va aller… sinon je pourrais
à la place t'entourer d'affection … inventer
des canapés de lumière
les installer bien soigneux dans le fond
d'accueil de mes chambres intérieures où je prie allongé contre
la tendresse du dasein ou tout autre impression de tiédeur

*

STÉPHANE BOUQUET

Les amours suivants, translated by Michelle Noteboom

These translations came out of a week-long translation seminar held at Reid Hall in Montparnasse, Paris, during June 2011, sponsored by the international arts association Tamaas. Poets worked in pairs so that each participant was both an author and a translator. Selections from each pair's work were subsequently published in a journal called *Read {a journal of inter-translation: 2011}* by Tamaas and 1913 Press.

II

In the metro I look up from the book and
oh… he's holding flowers not for me
and a cake box
not for me… once again a face is a dangerous
disembarkment of hope
e.g. we're not void of tomorrows…the proof you are
there… beginner on the cusp
of human acts and your fear of coming back
with no smiles… it'll be ok… or else instead
I could surround you with affection… invent
couches of light
and set them up carefully in the welcoming
recesses of my inner rooms where I pray lying against
the tenderness of dasein or any other impression of tepidity

*

IV

Chaque fois que j'embrasse le dealer…
du coup souvent interrompus
bipé urgence argent il doit partir il revient
… et chaque fois que je l'attends je pense aux
foules inouïes de gens qui se droguent…
heureusement il r'accourt toujours
presto vu la chimie de limaille
de nos peaux comme
si on était des séries de + / - concordants et nous
recommençons oh auj. ça serait immanence
sans condition du globe terrestre… moi qui avive son cou
… lui qui montre la capote
façon polie d'obtenir le droit de pénétrer
la liesse gémissant du lierre et du vent intérieurs

IV

Every time I kiss the dealer…
and so we often end up interrupted
beep hurry cash gotta go be right back
… and every time I wait for him I think of
the huge crowds of people using drugs…
luckily he always races back
pronto pulled by the iron chemistry
of our skins as
if we were a series of compatible + / –'s and we
start up again oh today it'd be unconditional
immanence of the planet earth… me kindling his neck
… him flashing the rubber
polite means of getting permission to penetrate
the blissful sighs of inner realms of ivy

V

Tee-shirt rouge et voix
voilée… on fait du yoga ensemble… beaucoup moins fort
que moi mais supérieurement plus beau…
à la fin dans shavasana quand on est censés devenir
une des vibrations quelconques de l'air et la cloche rituelle
nous dépose
presque derrière l'absence je peux seulement
penser avec mon animal de vivre oh la
la il y a cette longue mince envie
allongée à 2m si je me
roulais sur lui est-ce vraiment désormais la seule
espérance d'atténuer
à cause de la douceur dans tes os
la vitesse de mourir contre quoi je récite follement un autre rose
ce matin mignon

*

V

Red t-shirt and raspy
voice… we do yoga together… not nearly as good
as me but supremely better looking…
at the end in savasana when we're supposed to become
one of the various vibrations and the ritual bell
lies us down
almost behind absence I can only
think with my animal of life oh
wow there's this long slender desire
lying 6 ft away what if I
rolled onto it… is it really now the only
hope of slowing
'cause of the softness in your bones
the speed of death against which I crazily recite how to compare
you to a summer's day

*

X

Et puis après nous sommes partis
ensemble & en voiture il conduit…
le soleil glacé tape sur des villages peints gris bleu
… aucun parking surveillé
n'accepte les voitures 4 nuits d'affilée on ne peut pas
laisser / sauter dans le train qu'il adore… l'autoroute
est dégagée le gps en charge du trajet on parle de
la conférence sur le climat de cancun
ou de n'importe quoi qui a le son de sa voix
et voici le récit imprévu
… il était une fois 1&1
profite d'un peu de temps proche et d'air voisin
porté par une coque de métal elle aussi fragile
et si elle aussi facile à écraser

X

In the end we left
together by car & he drove…
he drives… the world sounds immediately better in the present
the icy sun beats on the villages painted grey blue
… no parking lot
agrees to take cars four nights in a row so we can't
leave / hop on the train he loves… he talks of things
like the climate conference in Cancun
the highway's empty gps guides the way
and suddenly a definition
of love in action transpires = 1&1
enjoys a little close time and shared air
borne in a metal shell which is fragile also
and so also easy to crash

PHILIPPE BECK

from *Opéradiques* (Paris: Flammarion, 2014)

MOTS GELÉS

Il y a pré-son comme il y a pré-danse.
Chacun est le Pilote Effrayé
au banquet flotté.
Il est parti de Papimanie.
Les sons ont le dessus battelé.
Le banquet flotté, divisant, parle
des immoraux de l'île : des mots dégèlent
sur le chemin de l'eau. Au pays du départ,
aucun feu ne chauffait luettes
ou langues empesées.
Les bouches étaient fermées
par un hiver bloqué.
A Intériorité d'air passé.
Raidies et froidies.
Mais, sur mer,
il y a des gens qui parlent en l'air ?
À côté du bateau ou sur lui ?
Ailleurs ? Navigués entendent
des sons épars.
Des pré-sons avant la danse
déglacée ? Dégelée ?
Qui bat la plaisante moquette ?
C'est la tête coupée d'Orphée
qui continue des plaintes nagées
stimulées de vents moyens ?
Navigant l'entend à côté comme en mai
1852 Thoreau entend
la scierie qui réduit la crue,

PHILIPPE BECK

from *Opéradiques*, translated by Emma Wagstaff

FROZEN WORDS

There is pre-sound as there is pre-dance.
Everyone is the Frightened Skipper
at the drifted banquet.
He set out from Papimania.
A peal of sounds has the upper hand.
The drifted, tippling banquet speaks
of the island's sinners : words thaw
on the waterway. In the country of origin
no fire warmed the starchy
throats or tongues.
Mouths were closed
by an obstructed winter.
To Inwardness of air past.
Rigid and colded.
But, at sea,
are there people who speak into the air?
Close by the boat or on it?
Elsewhere? Steeraged hear
scattered sounds.
Are they pre-sounds before
dancing thawed? Melted?
Who is it tapping a nice taunt?
Is it the severed head of Orpheus
who carries on the floating laments
prompted by enabling winds?
Steerer mishears it just as in May
1852 Thoreau heard
the sawing that reduced the spate

au son creux, galopant, déchireur,
cloche venue des nerfs de la poutre
travaillée.
(elle doit dompter les solives
comme un Orphée bruté
qui prépare des instruments ?)
Les paumes coiffent le pavillon tendu.
L'oreille hume l'air
comme une huître écaillée
qui entend des perles tressées
discourir dehors.
Femmes, enfants, hommes et chevaux
inaperçus
poussent des cris articulés.
Où ?
On dit : « À voiles et à rames ! »
pour fuir quoi ?
L'effrayé, son épée rouillée, rêve de cave
sans paroles,
comme de romance de terre,
loin de l'eau salée et d'Archer de Bagnolet,
et des parlants au fumier.
Pilote Calmant sait qu'au fond de la mer glacée
bataillent les « héros des mots »
(*Wallenstein*). Ils veulent trop.
Comme à Marignan
ou au pays des peaux de martres.
Tiques, torches et portes d'air…
L'hiver est leur âge d'explication.
Arismapiens (géants, Gargantuas borgnes)
et Nephelibates (ils passent
au milieu des neiges sombres qu'ils griffent

to the hollow, galloping, rending sound,
bell emerged wrung from the beam
in travail.
(must it train the joists
like a beasted Orpheus
crafting instruments?)
Palms cup the straining ear.
The ear sniffs the air
like an oyster
that hears threaded pearls
talking outside.
Women, children, men and horses
articulated cries
unnoticed.
Where?
They say, "To the sails and the oars!"
to escape what?
The fearful one, his sword rusted, dreams of a speechless
cellar,
and of a song of the earth,
far from the salt water and the Archer of Bagnolet,
and speakers on their dunghill.
Serene Skipper knows that at the bottom of the frozen sea
the "word heroes" fight
(*Wallenstein*). They want too much.
Just as at Marignan
or in the land of sable.
Ticks, torches and airy doors...
The winter is their age of explanation.
Arimaspians (giants, one-eyed Gargantuas)
and Nephelibates (they stamp
across the midst of the sombre snow that they paw

et tiennent pour des nuées alpines) ont
une guerre scolaire avec exclamations.
Masses, armures et peur d'attaque
se lancent dans l'hiver.
Les paroles gèlent en l'air sévère.
Sous l'œil des bêtes sphingées.
Après la rigueur du froid,
un temps libère les Gelées.
Les paroles fondent et des oreilles froides
se dressent au Dégel.
Comme au bord de la montagne
légale,
il y a des phrases encore congelées :
qui va les re-fouetter ?
Administrer la dégelée ?
Printemps est un bouclier ou un fouet ?
On voit les voix sensiblement.
Il y a de futures saisies au repas.
Les paroles glacées sont des dragées colorées.
On voit des mots de craie, des mots refaits,
des mots de gueule (plaisantés) ou d'azur,
des mots de sable,
des mots dorés, échauffés dans des mains ;
ils fondent comme neige. On les entend *réalement* :
mais c'est le babil des battus et perroquets,
des zézayants et des buttants, qui disent aussi,
dans des regrets du futur hiberné :
abbo – gabbo – babbo – Tebe – plebe – zebe –
converrebbe.
Il y a un bonbon plus gros,
qu'un incliné échauffe entre ses doigts :
il rend un son comme éclate un marron
au feu.

and take to be Alpine clouds) fight
a scholarly war with exclamations.
Armoured hordes and fear of attack
launch themselves into the winter.
Speech freezes in the harsh air.
Watched by sphinxed beasts.
After the cold's harshness,
a change frees the Frozen ones.
Speech melts and cold ears
prick up at the Thaw.
Since on the edge of the legal
mountain,
some sentences are still frozen :
who will whip them up again?
Give a good thawing?
Is Spring a shield or a whip?
You envision the voices.
There will be grabbing at table.
Frozen speech is pretty sugared almonds.
You see chalk words, remade words,
red-throated words (in jest) or azure words
sable words,
golden words, warmed up by hands ;
they melt like snow. You hear them *like real* :
but it's the babbling of losers and parrots,
of lispers and hit-men , who also say,
missing a hibernated future:
abbo – gabbo – babbo – Tebe – plebe – zebe –
converrebbe.
There's a bigger sweet
that a tilted one warms up with his fingers :
it brings up sounds like a chestnut popping
on the fire.

Flamme pousse le cri fondu
du coup de cannon
ou le chant du faucon d'avant.
Panurge veut des mots en supplément.
Pantagruel dit qu'amour donne des mots.
Il en vend ? Il fait parler de lui.
Le commerce des syllabes
est acte d'avocat ailé ? Et d'avocat faiseur
plutôt que vautour ?
(Jean Fabre acide l'avocat poseur
et plumant.)
Le silence est à vendre au premier temps ?
L'incliné jette encore des poignées
de futurs fondants, des perles d'hiver :
des paroles piquées,
des fendues retournées
à la guerre, proférées par gorge coupée,
saisissantes et détournantes.
Ensemble ranimées,
elles groupent les hin, hin, hin, hin,
his, ticque, torche, lorgne, brededin,
brededac, frr, frrr, frrr, bou, bou,
bou, bou, bou, bou, bou, bou,
traccc, trac, trr, trr, trr, trrr, trrrrrr,
on, on, on, on ououououon,
comme transpose l'*Ekri Rabelais*.
Avec hennissements
à l'heure qu'on choque.
D'autres bruits, dégelant rendent des sons
de tambours, fifres, clairons, trompes,
chalumeaux et sacs à vent.
Miaulements sont des interventions

Flame emits the melted cry
of canon fire
or the song of an old field-piece.
Panurge wants extra words.
Pantagruel says love gives words.
Is he selling any? Everyone talks about him.
Is the trade in syllables
a deed of a winged lawyer? And of a lawyer who makes
and not a vulture?
(acid Jean Fabre posing and fleecing
lawyer.)
Is silence for sale in a first instance?
The tilted one is still throwing handfuls
of melting futures, winter pearls:
nicked speech,
cracked ones returned
to war, offered up by cut throat,
striking and diverting.
Brought back to life together,
they gather some hin, hin, hin, hins
his, ticks, torches, eyes, brededins,
brededacks, frr, frrr, frrrs, bou, bou,
bou, bou, bou, bou, bou, bous,
tracck, tracks, trr, trr, trr, trrr, trrrrrrs,
on, on, on, on ouououououons,
just as set down by *Writ Rabelais*
With whinnying
at the moment of clashing.
Other noises, thawing, give out sounds
of drums, fifes, clarions, horns,
pipes and bagpipes
Caterwauling is argument

d'arguments
(avalisque, babou, ailes aux joues
équipant). La guerre a bien amusé ?
Elle a détourné le bloqué.
Glacé les rubans.
L'embouteillage des mots
de gueule et la garde des devises
de fête dans de l'huile
comme on garde neige et glace
hors du temps
perdent le sens :
comme l'homme réserve
ce qui ne manque pas et se donne
chaque jour avec bruit,
mots gueulés ou déglacés,
dépliés au Murmure Rampé.
Mais du Manoir de Vérité,
des mots ou des idées sont tombés
comme on tombe d'hiver ?
Ou d'automne préparatoire ?
Les voltigeantes et les volantes,
le lien de poisson-moine et de grain véhément,
les associés,
ont habité un bâtiment éternisé ?
Comme des trombes ou la rosée
tombée sur la toison de Gédéon ?
Vues, revues, lues, relues,
paperassées et feuilletées, comme compulsoires
et déclinatoires, etc. Les inclusions
concentrées, les ronds dans l'eau qui font parler,
et redémarrer des passions publiées,
avec les bouches suscitées et écaillées.

in action
(avalisque, grimace, put to sea on winged
cheeks). Was the war fun?
It diverted the one frozen-in.
Iced the ribbons.
The stoppage of red-throated
words and the keeping of festival
mottos in oil
just like keeping snow and ice
outside time
lose their meaning:
just as man keeps
what is not lacking and gives himself
every day noisily,
throaty or thawed words,
unfolded to the Crawling Murmur.
But out of the Manor of Truth,
did words or ideas fall
as one falls from winter?
Or readying autumn?
The fluttering and flying ones,
linking monkfish and violent grain,
the associates,
did they live in a never-ending building?
Like torrents or the dew
on Gideon's fleece?
Seen, reseen, read, reread,
paperworked and flicked through, as if consultive
and declinative, etc. Concentrated
ripples, balls in the water that compel speech,
and the resurgence of published passions,
mouths kindled and scaled.

La musique est comme les paroles gelées ?
On ne sait d'où elle vient ?
Où elle est ?
Elle archive des guerres dans l'air.
Comme trompette et cor.
Les sons dehors continuent les Palabrés,
et les échos de la plaine
tombent au sol. Pré-aérienne, une course
de poussières sphériques a débuté.
La harpe de silence est bougée,
avec le perce-bois et le grillon.
Pour des contretemps
et les heroïsmes notés.
Il faut un sonnet brûleur
pour chanter l'ampoule de vent
rauque et croassant de nuit
et l'effet de la pompe grinçant
dans la galerie terrée ?
Une satire en mesure dans la vallée ?
Oui : pour éprouver la fibre dure de l'air.
Le clavier grince comme balançoire
et continue le télégraphe,
harpiste du vent communicant.
Des sons montent, fumée
et chapeau cloche des pompes
dedans, tente où habite l'Inquiet,
le désincliné.
Ils font aussi des bulles de brouillard,
d'amples perles de vin entêté
et automné.
Le brouillard s'habille aussi,
rhabille écume douce

Music is like frozen speech?
Do we not know where it comes from?
Where it is?
It archives wars in the air.
As do the trumpet and the horn.
Outdoor sounds pursue the Debated,
and echoes from the plain
fall to earth. Pre-airborne, a spherical
dust race has got underway.
The harp of silence is moved
with the woodworm and the cricket.
For disputes
and heroic deeds noted.
Is a burning sonnet needed
to sing of a phial of wind
rough and croaking by night
and the effect of a creaking pump
in the earthed-up gallery?
A scored satire in the valley?
Yes: to test the hard fibre of the air.
The keyboard creaks like swing
and on goes the telegraph,
harpist of the communicating wind.
Sounds rise, smoke
and pumps' cloche hats
inside, tent where the Worried one lives
the untilted one.
They also make bubbles of fog,
generous pearls of stubborn autumned
wine.
The fog dresses itself too,
reclothes gentle foam

dont l'air fuité se dégage. (La fuite est cavée.)
D'où la harpe parlante, débrumée.
Il y a dans la pensée
des accords qui passent des oratoires ?
Thoreau le croit.
Et les harpes parlées de maintenant ?
Elles en pensent quoi ?
Enfant réalisant a des idées
là-dessus.

from which the leaked air frees itself. (The leak is caved.)
Hence the speaking harp, unmisted.
Are there in thought
chords that surpass oratories?
Thoreau thought so.
And the present spoken harps?
What do they think?
Realising child has ideas
about that.

SANDRA MOUSSEMPÈS

from *Sunny Girls* (Paris: Poésie/Flammarion, 2015)

Tout avait commencé par une phrase satisfaisante
De petites rivières qui pensent à ce que l'on dit d'elles

Mais étalées dans le temps et craintives
Puis un langage creux avait terni cette vague idée de certitude

Une attitude tout aussi contractée par la maladresse & le désir vif
Ce sont mes propres ceintures à base de myrtille que l'on adapte ici

Avec le détachement d'une enfance réelle ou d'une cuisse de poulet frit

*

SANDRA MOUSSEMPÈS

Sunny Girls, translated by Eléna Rivera

Everything began with a satisfying phrase
Little rivers imagine what is said of them

But spread out in time and timid
Then empty language tarnished this vague idea of certainty

An attitude just as taut because of its clumsiness & strong desire
These are my own blueberry tinged cinctures that one adapts here

With the detachment of a real childhood or of a fried chicken thigh

*

CULTE

Certaines princesses sur le tard ont pour obligation de placer chaque jour dans leur pensée, une expression d'orfèvre comme « retour à la normale »

Les forêts emmêlées à leurs pieds sont des joies quotidiennes rarement volées par une sorcière

De plus en plus les princesses se canonisent au vernis à ongle vert dépréciant ainsi toute forme de revanche

Non
est la nouvelle définition de
stop
remplaçant fourchettes borderline
& peur de peur de

CULT

Certain princesses who came to it late in life have an obligation
every day to place in their thoughts a sterling expression like
"return to normal"

Entangled forests at their feet are daily joys rarely stolen by
a witch

Increasingly princesses become canonized with green nail polish
in this way belittling all forms of revenge

No
is the new definition of
stop
replacing psychotic forks
& fear of fear of

En réarrangeant une fiction d'oubliées
par inclination universelle

et non des corn-flakes ramollis par le lait
le passage vers le passé le passé vers le langage

un problème trop fourbe pour être pris au sérieux
les atténuations de Walser et son demi-tiret

comme si relire éternellement le même passage d'un livre
sous-tend racheter les fonctions curatives du présent

la norme n'est plus ce qu'elle était
ni même quand la piscine gonflable entravait l'allée

au lieu de vous disséquer
je vous donnerai une leçon de skateboard vous m'apporterez les roues

fini les ratures ici on ne se découpe pas au pochoir
on ne s'étale pas sur du pur grenat

*

Arranging again a fiction of forgotten women
by a universal tendency

and not some cornflakes softened by milk
the passage toward the past the past toward language

a problem too treacherous to be taken seriously
the toning down of Walser and his half-dash

as if eternally rereading the same passage of a book
would buy back the healing powers of the present

the norm is not what was
not even when the inflatable pool hampered the hall

instead of dissecting you
I will give you a skateboarding lesson you'll bring me the wheels

finished with corrections here one isn't cut to stencil
one doesn't spread oneself on pure garnet

*

Je me souviens de la maison sculptée

Je me souviens du drame anglais, ce rêve de fin de nuit
J'étais dans une maison divisée en trois, j'écoutais les conseils
d'un jeune polonais aux cheveux noirs

Hauteur des cieux et des solitudes durables
Au moins tu es sûr de celle-là

Ce n'est pas une version éthérée malgré son témoignage
Ces femmes s'avéraient dans le réel être un seul homme

De ce corps ciselé, de ce visage d'ange brun subsistait la sensation
d'ivresse.
Mais tout était lié à l'envergure de son déploiement, il me fallait le
croire pour le voir.

Depuis je pense toujours aux maisons sculptées, c'est un travail
en cours qui me rend passive mais pas désarmée.

Je me suis attachée à la vérité
Je suis attachée à la vérité

Il y a une transgression, un magasin de musique
Tous deux s'entrouvrent à leur façon

I remember the sculpted house

I remember the English drama, that late night-dream
I was in a house divided in three, I listened to the advice of a young Pole with black hair

Height of heavens and enduring solitudes.
At least you are sure of that one.

It isn't an ethereal version despite its testimony
These women proved to be in reality only one man

From this chiseled body, from this brown angel face remained the sensation of intoxication
But it was all tied to the wingspan's unfolding, I needed to see it to believe it.

Since then I always think of sculpted houses, it's a work-in-progress that renders me passive but not disarmed.

I attached myself to the truth
I am attached to the truth

There's a transgression, a music store
Both openings in their way

GILLES ORTLIEB

Meuse Métal, etc. (Le temps qu'il fait, 2005)

Ode (pour traverser les jours sans maugréer)

à la petite tasse émaillée, au rebord bleuté,
dont le métal brûle lorsque, par distraction,
on la saisit non par l'anse, mais par les côtés.
Compagne des débuts de nuit et des travaux
en cours, jamais très éloignée du *Nouveau
dictionnaire analogique* de Niobey sur quoi
il lui arrive d'être posée – et qui veille seule
au milieu des objets, à la température exacte
de la pièce, avant de resservir le lendemain
et les lendemains des lendemains, intacte.

GILLES ORTLIEB

Meuse Métal, etc., translated by Stephen Romer

Ode (for getting through the days without whinging)

to the little enamel cup, with the blue-tinted edge
and the metal that burns, if you seize it
distractedly by the sides and not the handle.
Companion of the night-shift, of the works
in progress, never too far from the Niobey
Nouveau dictionnaire analogique on which
it is sometimes placed — it sits on alone
amongst the objects, at the exact temperature
of the room, before being used next morning,
and the morning after the morning after, intact.

Par la fenêtre, un petit homme en cache-col bronze et chapeau de feutre grisâtre, flanqué d'un quadrupède au poil plus miel que roux, et qui escorte chacun de ses pas. L'étonnant est que tous les deux s'immobilisent parfois longuement, malgré le froid, pour ausculter le ciel ou en dévisager les abords immédiats, regardant passer les voitures et les suivant des yeux jusqu'au tournant, puis pivotant de trois-quarts pour jouir d'un autre angle de vue, avant – à l'issue d'une station plus prolongée encore que d'habitude (admirable patience du chien, qui feint de s'intéresser aussi à ce presque rien dont il est témoin) – de se résigner à rentrer, à pas prudents que le verglas étrécit. Et quand on les croit disparus, ils sont là de nouveau, en faction, l'homme au couvre-chef gris et son renard miniature au poil moins roux que blond, qui emboîte chaque demi-pas de son compagnon.

Through the window a little man in a bronze scarf
and a grey felt hat, is flanked by a quadruped
more honey-coloured than russet, who escorts
his every step. The astonishing thing is how
the two of them stop dead sometimes, for long
intervals, and in spite of the cold, to scrutinize
the heavens or their immediate surroundings,
watching the cars go by until they reach the corner,
and then the two of them swivel three-quarters round
to enjoy a further view, before, emerging from a longer
freeze even than usual (wonderful patience of the dog,
who pretends to take an interest in the quasi
non-events he witnesses) – they resolve to go home,
footsteps reduced by the ice. And when you think
they've gone, there they are again, in league,
the man with the grey hat, and the miniature fox,
with a coat more blond than russet, who follows
in his companion's every semi-footstep.

GILLES ORTLIEB

Le Train des jours (Bordeaux: Finitude, 2010)

GRUES ET FUMÉES

Visibles ce matin de la fenêtre comme chaque matin,
quelques ouvriers en tenue orange, casqués, et occupés
à démouler, étage après étage, l'immeuble neuf qui
s'élèvera bientôt à la place de l'ancien cinéma *Victory*,
détruit. À mi-distance, tendue sous un auvent de zinc
branlant, et remuant tout juste sous les coups de vent,
une serviette couleur bleu roi, évoquant assez une toile
de Thomas Jones intitulée, si je ne me trompe pas,
Un mur à Naples ; et une volute de fumée s'échappant
avec un débit variable d'un conduit parallélépipédique
débouchant, rouge brique, parmi des toitures en pente.
Voici donc pour les choses aperçues en mouvement
aujourd'hui : le gris d'une fumée, un menu rectangle
bleuté et les déplacements huilés, tout à fait silencieux,
de deux grues jumelles détourant leurs armatures jaunes
contre le ciel brouillé – sans oublier les blocs de béton
énormes dont elles sont lestées, et qu'il est impossible
de ne pas imaginer chutant au milieu des passants, ou
sur des carrosseries de voitures aussi faciles à froisser
que du papier aluminium entre les mains d'un marmiton.
Grues et fumées : elles me paraissent assez bien figurer,
tandis que je les observe alternativement, deux principes
qui nous sont, d›une certaine manière, inhérents : le dur
et le gazeux, le rigide et le volatil, le solide et l'inconstant
autrement dit le jaune et le blanc, l'eau et le fer, la plume
dans le vent, et ce qui a été bâti pour lui résister sans plier.

GILLES ORTLIEB

Le Train des jours, translated by Stephen Romer
(published in *Poetry Review*, 103, 2 (Summer 2013), p. 81)

CRANES AND SMOKE

Visible this morning through the window, like every morning,
a group of labourers in hard-hats and orange overalls, engaged in
freeing, like a multi-storied cake from its mould, the brand new
tower-block, rising where the old *Victory* cinema used to be,
now gone. In the middle distance, spread out below an unsteady
zinc awning, and stirring very slightly in the gusts of wind,
a royal-blue towel, that strongly brings to mind a painting by
Thomas Jones entitled, if I'm not mistaken, *A Wall in Naples.*
There's a scroll of smoke of variable outflow escaping from a
parallelepiped conduit, poking up from amongst the angled roofs.
This, then, is the gist of things perceived to be in movement today:
grey smoke, a small blue rectangle, and the well-oiled, absolutely
silent movements of two twin cranes, whose yellow armature
is thrown into relief against the clotted sky – not forgetting
their attachments, two huge blocks of concrete ballast, whose
only-too-imaginable-fall would scrumple the cars below
like a sheet of tinfoil between the hands of a baker's boy.
Cranes and smoke: observing the one and then the other,
they seem to figure twin principles, both of them in some sense
intrinsic to us: the hard and the vaporous, the rigid and the volatile,
the solid and the flighty; or in other words yellow and white,
iron and water, the feather in the wind, and the thing constructed
to resist the wind unyieldingly. Cloud and breath, condensations
and exhalations, and against them, the home-grown machinery
with its cogs meshed. Both principles, what's more, exhibit
a similar kind of resistance, to the seasons and the weekly cycle,

Ou encore la nuée, la buée, les vapeurs, les exhalaisons
et, d'un autre côté, la mécanique engrenée, faite maison.
Les unes et les autres montrant d'ailleurs une résistance
analogue, survivant aux saisons et au bal des semaines,
guère menacées dans leur existence et peu menaçantes.
Grues et fumées aux mouvements gratuits ou calculés,
compagnie accoutumée de jours, comme elles, partagés
entre la construction et la déperdition, entre le ciment
et la dissolution: double exemple à suivre, absolument.

their existence on the whole unthreatened and unthreatening. Cranes and smoke, with their movements random or calculated, habitual accompaniment to days that are, like them, divided between building and dispersal, cementing and coming loose, both after their fashion exemplary, and hence to be followed.

JEAN-MICHEL ESPITALLIER

Salle des machines (Paris: Flammarion, 2015)

HISTOIRES DE JUSQU'À 15

Histoire de jusqu'à 15 (version tronquée)
1 (un), 2 (deux), 3 (trois), 4 (quatre), 5 (cinq), 6 (six), 7 (sept), 8 (huit), 9 (neuf), 10 (dix), 11 (onze), 12 (douze), 13 (treize), 14 (quatorze).

Histoire de jusqu'à 15 (version corrigée)
1 (un), 2 (deux), 3 (trois), 4 (quatre), 5 (cinq), 6 (six), 7 (sept), 8 (huit), 9 (neuf), 10 (dix), 11 (onze), 12 (douze), 13 (treize), 14 (quatorze), 15 (quinze).

Histoire de jusqu'à 15 (version abrégée)
(…), 15 (quinze).

Histoire de jusqu'à 15 (version superstitieuse)
1 (un), 2 (deux), 3 (trois), 4 (quatre), 5 (cinq), 6 (six), 7 (sept), 8 (huit), 9 (neuf), 10 (dix), 11 (onze), 12 (douze), 12bis (douze bis), 14 (quatorze), 15 (quinze).

Histoire de jusqu'à 15 (version à rebours – extrait)
(…) 40 (quarante), 39 (trente-neuf), 38 (trente-huit), 37 (trente-sept), 36 (trente-six), 35 (trente-cinq), 34 (trente-quatre), 33 (trente-trois), 32 (trente-deux), 31 (trente et un), 30 (trente), 29 (vingt-neuf), 28 (vingt-huit), 27 (vingt-sept), 26 (vingt-six), 25 (vingt-cinq), 24 (vingt-quatre), 23 (vingt-trois), 22 (vingt-deux), 21 (vingt et un), 20 (vingt), 19 (dix-neuf), 18 (dix-huit), 17 (dix-sept), 16 (seize), 15 (quinze).

JEAN-MICHEL ESPITALLIER

Salle des machines, translated by Keston Sutherland

TALES OF UP TO 15

Tale of up to 15 (truncated version)

1 (one), 2 (two), 3 (three), 4 (four), 5 (five), 6 (six), 7 (seven),
8 (eight), 9 (nine), 10 (ten), 11 (eleven), 12 (twelve), 13 (thirteen),
14 (fourteen).

Tale of up to 15 (corrected version)

1 (one), 2 (two), 3 (three), 4 (four), 5 (five), 6 (six), 7 (seven),
8 (eight), 9 (nine), 10 (ten), 11 (eleven), 12 (twelve), 13 (thirteen),
14 (fourteen), 15 (fifteen).

Tale of up to 15 (abridged version)

(…), 15 (fifteen).

Tale of up to 15 (superstitious version)

1 (one), 2 (two), 3 (three), 4 (four), 5 (five), 6 (six), 7 (seven),
8 (eight), 9 (nine), 10 (ten), 11 (eleven), 12 (twelve), 12 (repeat)
(twelve (repeat)), 14 (fourteen), 15 (fifteen).

Tale of up to 15 (retroversion)

(…) 40 (forty), 39 (thirty-nine), 38 (thirty-eight), 37 (thirty-seven),
36 (thirty-six), 35 (thirty-five), 34 (thirty-four), 33 (thirty-three),
32 (thirty-two), 31 (thirty-one), 30 (thirty), 29 (twenty-nine),
28 (twenty-eight), 27 (twenty-seven), 26 (twenty-six),
25 (twenty-five), 24 (twenty-four), 23 (twenty-three),
22 (twenty-two), 21 (twenty-one), 20 (twenty), 19 (nineteen),
18 (eighteen), 17 (seventeen), 16 (sixteen), 15 (fifteen).

Histoire de jusqu'à 15 (version ratée)
1 (un), 2 (deux), 3 (trois), 4 (quatre), 5 (cinq), 6 (six), 7 (sept), 8 (huit), 9 (neuf), 10 (dix), 11 (onze), 12 (douze), 13 (treize), 14 (quatorze), 16 (seize).

Histoire de jusqu'à 15 (version dyslexique)
1 (un), 2 (deux), 3 (trois), 4 (quatre), 5 (cinq), 6 (six), 7 (sept), 8 (huit), 9 (neuf), 10 (dix), 11 (onze), 12 (douze), 13 (treize), 14 (quatorze), 51 (quinze).

Histoire de jusqu'à 15 (version feignasse)
Na-na-na-na-na-na-na-na, 15 (quinze).

Histoire de jusqu'à 15 (version bordélique/ disjonctive)
1 (deux), 2 (treize), 3 (un), 4 (onze), 5 (quatorze), 6 (dix), 7 (neuf), 8 (quinze), 9 (douze), 10 (trois), 11 (cinq), 12 (six), 13 (huit), 14 (sept), 15 (quatre).

Histoire de jusqu'à 15 (ordre alphabétique – hommage à Claude Closky)
Cinq (5), deux (2), dix (10), douze (12), huit (8), neuf (9), onze (11), quatorze (14), quatre (4), quinze (15), sept (7), six (6), treize (13), trois (3), un (1)

Histoire de jusqu'à 15 (version militaire)
1 (un) / 2 (deux), 1 (un) / 2 (deux), 1 (un) / 2 (deux), 1 (un) / 2 (deux), 1 (un) / 2 (deux), 1 (un) / 2 (deux), 1 (un) / 2 (deux), 15 (quinze).

Histoire de jusqu'à 15 (version départementale)
Ain, Aisne, Allier, Alpes-de-Haute-Provence, Hautes-Alpes, Alpes-Maritimes, Ardèche, Ardennes, Ariège, Aube, Aude, Aveyron, Bouches-du-Rhône, Calvados, 15 (quinze).

Tale of up to 15 (failed version)

1 (one), 2 (two), 3 (three), 4 (four), 5 (five), 6 (six), 7 (seven), 8 (eight), 9 (nine), 10 (ten), 11 (eleven), 12 (twelve), 13 (thirteen), 14 (fourteen), 16 (sixteen).

Tale of up to 15 (dyslexic version)

1 (one), 2 (two), 3 (three), 4 (four), 5 (five), 6 (six), 7 (seven), 8 (eight), 9 (nine), 10 (ten), 11 (eleven), 12 (twelve), 13 (thirteen), 14 (fourteen), 51 (fifteen).

Tale of up to 15 (bluffer's guide version)

Na-na-na-na-na-na-na-na, 15 (fifteen).

Tale of up to 15 (linguistically innovative/disjunctive version)

1 (two), 2 (thirteen), 3 (one), 4 (eleven), 5 (fourteen), 6 (ten), 7 (nine), 8 (fifteen), 9 (twelve), 10 (three), 11 (five), 12 (six), 13 (eight), 14 (seven), 15 (four).

Tale of up to 15 (in alphabetic order – in homage to Claude Closky)

Eight (8), eleven (11), fifteen (15), five (5), four (4), fourteen (14), nine (9), one (1), seven (7), six (6), ten (10), thirteen (13), three (3), twelve (12), two (2).

Tale of up to 15 (military version)

1 (one) / 2 (two), 1 (one) / 2 (two), 1 (one) / 2 (two), 1 (one) / 2 (two), 1 (one) / 2 (two), 1 (one) / 2 (two), 1 (one) / 2 (two), 15 (fifteen).

Tale of up to 15 (counties version)

Bath and North East Somerset, Bedfordshire, Berkshire, Blackpool, Blackburn with Darwen, Bournemouth, Brighton and Hove, Bristol, Buckinghamshire, Cambridgeshire, Cheshire, Cumbria, Darlington, Derby, 15 (fifteen).

Histoire de jusqu'à 15 (version alphabétique)

a, b, c, d, e, f, g, h, i, j, k, l, m, n, 15 (quinze).

Histoire de jusqu'à 15 (version polyglotte)

1 (ein), 2 (due), 3 (nett), 4 (patru), 5 (pyaht), 6 (sitta), 7 (shtate), 8 (oito), 9 (nau), 10 (shi), 11 (eleven), 12 (twaalf), 13 (djioù-san), 14 (catorce), 15 (quinze).

Histoire de jusqu'à 15 (version latine)

I (unus), II (duo), III (tres), IV (quattuor), V (quinque), VI (sex), VII (septem), VIII (octo), IX (novem), X (decem), XI (undecim), XII (duodecim), XIII (tredecim), XIV (quattuor decim), 15 (quinze).

Histoire de jusqu'à 15 (version mai 2007)

Mardi, mercredi, jeudi, vendredi, samedi, dimanche, lundi, mardi, mercredi, jeudi, vendredi, samedi, dimanche, lundi, 15 (quinze).

Histoire de jusqu'à 15 (version monomaniaque)

15 (quinze), 15 (quinze), 15 (quinze), 15 (quinze), 15 (quinze), 15 (quinze), 15 (quinze), 15 (quinze), 15 (quinze), 15 (quinze), 15 (quinze), 15 (quinze), 15 (quinze), 15 (quinze), 15 (quinze).

Histoire de jusqu'à 15 (version morse)

. - - - -, . . - - -, . . . - -, ... -, ..., - . . . ., - - . . ., - - - . ., - - - - ., . - - - - -
- - - -, . - - - - . - - - -, . - - - - . . - - -, . - - - - . . . - -, . - - - - . . . . -,
15 (quinze)

Tale of up to 15 (alphabetic version)
a, b, c, d, e, f, g, h, i, j, k, l, m, n, 15 (fifteen).

Tale of up to 15 (polyglot version)
1 (ein), 2 (due), 3 (nett), 4 (patru), 5 (pyaht), 6 (sitta), 7 (shtate), 8 (oito), 9 (nau), 10 (shi), 11 (onze), 12 (twaalf), 13 (djioù-san), 14 (catorce), 15 (fifteen).

Tale of up to 15 (latin version)
I (unus), II (duo), III (tres), IV (quattuor), V (quinque), VI (sex), VII (septem), VIII (octo), IX (novem), X (decem), XI (undecim), XII (duodecim), XIII (tredecim), XIV (quattuor decim), 15 (fifteen).

Tale of up to 15 (April 2008 version)
Tuesday, Wednesday, Thursday, Friday, Saturday, Sunday, Monday, Tuesday, Wednesday, Thursday, Friday, Saturday, Sunday, Monday, 15 (fifteen).

Tale of up to 15 (monomaniac version)
15 (fifteen), 15 (fifteen), 15 (fifteen), 15 (fifteen), 15 (fifteen), 15 (fifteen), 15 (fifteen), 15 (fifteen), 15 (fifteen), 15 (fifteen), 15 (fifteen), 15 (fifteen), 15 (fifteen), 15 (fifteen), 15 (fifteen).

Tale of up to 15 (morse version)
. - - - -, . . - - -, . . . - -, ... -, ..., - . . . ., - - . . ., - - - . ., - - - - ., . - - - - -
- - - -, . - - - - . - - - -, . - - - - . . - - -, . - - - - . . . - -, . - - - - . . . . -,
15 (fifteen).

Histoire de jusqu'à 15 (version codes produits Leclerc)
Epicerie, liquides, fruits et légumes, droguerie, bazar, audio vidéo photo, textile, chaussures, crèmerie, fromage à la coupe, surgelés, boulangerie, pâtisserie, boucherie, 15 (quinze).

Histoire de jusqu'à 15 (version RATP)
Château de Vincennes-La Défense, Nation-Porte Dauphine, Galliéni-Pont de Levallois, Porte de Clignancourt-Porte d'Orléans, Bobigny Pablo Picasso-Place d'Italie, Nation-Charles de Gaulle Etoile, La Courneuve-Villejuif Louis Aragon/Mairie d'Ivry, Créteil-Balard, Mairie de Montreuil-Pont de Sèvres, Gare d'Austerlitz-Boulogne Pont de Saint-Cloud, Mairie des Lilas-Châtelet, Porte de La Chapelle-Mairie d'Issy, Gabriel Péri Asnières Gennevilliers/Saint-Denis Basilique-Châtillon Montrouge, Saint-Lazare-Bibliothèque François Mitterrand, 15 (quinze).

Histoire de jusqu'à 15 (version à l'envers)
14 (quatorze), 13 (treize), 12 (douze), 11 (onze), 10 (dix), 9 (neuf), 8 (huit), 7 (sept), 6 (six), 5 (cinq), 4 (quatre), 3 (trois), 2 (deux), 1 (un), 15 (quinze).

Histoire de jusqu'à 15 (version atomique)
Hydrogène, hélium, lithium, bérylium, bore, carbone, azote, oxygène, fluor, néon, sodium, magnésium, aluminium, silicium, 15 (quinze).

Histoire de jusqu'à 15 (version suite de Fibonacci)
1, 2, 3, 5, 8, 13, 21, 55, 89, 184, 233, 377, 610, 987, 15 (quinze).

Tale of up to 15 (veterinary services product codes version)
Antlers in Velvet from Any Country, Swine Hides for Trophies from Countries Affected with ASF, Approved Warehouse, Feathers for Commercial Use, Bovine Gall Stones, Bones, Horns, Ivory, Antlers, etc. for Other than Trophies, Bones, Skulls, Horns, Ivory, Antlers, etc. for Trophies, Bone Storage, Birds or Bird Capes or Mounts for Trophies, Casein, Lactalbumin, Lactose Hydrolysat, & Caseinates, Casein Storage, Cold Storage Warehouse, Restricted Hides & Skins for Tanning at a Commercial Tannery, Dry Milk Powder, 15 (fifteen).

Tale of up to 15 (tube version)
Victoria, St. James's Park, Westminster, Embankment, Charing Cross, Leicester Square, Tottenham Court Road, Goodge Street, Warren Street, Euston, Mornington Crescent, Camden Town, Chalk Farm, Belsize Park, 15 (fifteen).

Tale of up to 15 (backwards version)
14 (fourteen), 13 (thirteen), 12 (twelve), 11 (eleven), 10 (ten), 9 (nine), 8 (eight), 7 (seven), 6 (six), 5 (five), 4 (four), 3 (three), 2 (two), 1 (one), 15 (fifteen).

Tale of up to 15 (atomic version)
Hydrogen, helium, lithium, berylium, boron, carbon, nitrogen, oxygen, fluorine, neon, sodium, magnesium, aluminium, silicon, 15 (fifteen).

Tale of up to 15 (Fibonacci sequence version)
1, 2, 3, 5, 8, 13, 21, 55, 89, 184, 233, 377, 610, 987, 15 (fifteen).

Histoires de jusqu'à 15 (version anniversaire de mariage)

Noces de coton, noces de cuir, noces de froment, noces de cire, noces de bois, noces de chypre, noces de laine, noces de coquelicot, noces de faïence, noces d'étain, noce de corail, noces de soie, noces de muguet, noces de plomb, 15 (quinze).

Histoire de jusqu'à 15 (version cartes à jouer)

As, deux, trois, quatre, cinq, six, sept, huit, neuf, dix, valet, dame, roi, joker, 15 (quinze).

Histoire de jusqu'à 15 (version arrondissements de Paris)

Louvre, Bourse, Temple, Hôtel de Ville, Panthéon, Luxembourg, Palais Bourbon, Elysée, Opéra, Enclos Saint-Laurent, Popincourt, Reuilly, Gobelins, Observatoire, 15 (quinze).

Histoire de jusqu'à 15 (version Wingdings)

🗁 🕿◆■✆📪 🗎 🕿♎♏◆⌧✆📪 🗏
🕿⧫❒□♓⬧✆📪 🗐 🕿❑◆♋⧫❒♏✆📪 🗄
🕿♍♓■❑✆📪 ⌛ 🕿⬧♓⌧✆📪 🖮 🕿⬧♏◻⧫✆📪
🖰 🕿♒◆♓⧫✆📪 🖲 🕿■♏◆♐✆📪 🗁🗀
🕿♎♓⌧✆📪 🗁🗁 🕿□■⌘♏✆📪 🗁🗎
🕿♎□◆⌘♏✆📪 🗁🗏 🕿⧫❒♏♓⌘♏✆📪 🗁🗐
🕿❑◆♋⧫□❒⌘♏✆📪 🗁🗄 🕿❑◆♓■⌘♏✆📭

Tale of up to 15 (wedding anniversaries version)
Paper, cotton, leather, linen, wood, iron, copper, bronze, willow, aluminium, steel, silk, lace, ivory, 15 (fifteen).

Tale of up to 15 (playing cards version)
Ace, two, three, four, five, six, seven, eight, nine, ten, knight, queen, king, joker, 15 (fifteen).

Tale of up to 15 (London boroughs version)
City of Westminster, Kensington and Chelsea, Hammersmith and Fulham, Wandsworth, Lambeth, Southwark, Tower Hamlets, Hackney, Islington, Camden, Brent, Ealing, Hounslow, Richmond upon Thames, 15 (fifteen).

Tale of up to 15 (wingdings version)
📂 ☎□■♏✆📪 📄 ☎⧫⬥□✆📪 🗏 ☎⧫♒❒♏♏✆📪 🗐 ☎♐□◆❒✆📪 🗄 ☎♐♓❖♏✆📪 ⌛ ☎⬧♓⌧✆📪 🖮 ☎⬧♏❖♏■✆📪 🖰 ☎♏♓♑♒⧫✆📪 🖲 ☎■♓■♏✆📪 📂📁 ☎⧫♏■✆📪 📂📂 ☎♏●♏❖♏■✆📪 📂📄 ☎⧫⬥♏●❖♏✆📪 📂🗏 ☎⧫♒♓❒⧫♏♏■✆📪 📂🗐 ☎♐□◆❒⧫♏♏■✆📪 📂🗄 ☎♐♓♐⧫♏♏■✆🖎

—Je t'aime.
—Moi aussi.
—Je sais.
—Je sais que tu le sais.
—Je sais que tu sais que je sais que tu le sais.
—Et moi je sais que tu sais que je t'aime.
—Je sais que tu le sais et tu sais que je sais que tu sais que je le sais, et tu sais que je sais que tu sais que je t'aime.
—Je sais que tu le sais et tu sais que je sais que tu sais que je sais que tu sais que je t'aime, et je sais que tu sais que je sais que tu sais que je sais que tu le sais.
—Et tu aimes que je le sache ?
—Oui, j'aime savoir que tu le sais, j'aime que tu saches que je sais que tu m'aimes, j'aime savoir que tu m'aimes et j'aime savoir que tu le sais.
—Et moi j'aime savoir que tu sais que je sais que tu aimes savoir que je t'aime.
—Je sais et j'aime aimer savoir que tu aimes savoir que tu saches que je sais que tu sais que j'aime aimer savoir que tu saches que je sais que tu m'aimes.
—J'aime savoir t'aimer.
—J'aime aimer savoir que tu saches aimer que je sache t'aimer.
—J'aime savoir que tu aimes savoir que je le sache.
—Et moi j'aime aimer que tu aimes le savoir.
—Je sais que tu m'aimes et j'aime savoir que tu sais que je le sais.
—Je t'aime.
—Je sais.
—Je le savais.

HISTORY OF AMOROUS DISCOURSE

—I love you.
—Me too.
—I know.
—I know that you know.
—I know that you know that I know that you know.
—And for my part I know that you know that I love you.
—I know that you know and you know that I know that you know that I know, and you know that I know that you know that I love you.
—I know that you know and you know that I know that you know that I know that you know that I love you, and I know that you know that I know that you know that I know that you know.
—And do you love it that I know?
—Yes, I love knowing that you know, I love it that you know that I know that you love me, I love knowing that you love me and I love knowing that you know.
—And for my part I love knowing that you know that I know that you love knowing that I love you.
—I know and I love loving knowing that you love knowing that you know that I know that you know that I love loving knowing that you know that I love it that you love me.
—I love knowing to love you.
—I love loving knowing that you know to love it that I know to love you.
—I love knowing that you love knowing that I know.
—And for my part I love loving that you love to know.
—I know that you love me and I love knowing that you know that I know.
—I love you.
—I know.
—I knew it.

ABOUT THE POETS AND TRANSLATORS

Pierre Alferi, born in 1963, is the author of some twelve books of poetry as well as five novels and twenty short films. A frequent collaborator with musicians and visual artists, he has worked extensively to develop the genre of the cinépoème and the short lyric film. He is also the translator of a wide range of writers, from John Donne to George Oppen, and the co-founder of two literary journals, *Détail*, with Suzanne Doppelt, and *La Revue de Littérature Générale*, with Olivier Cadiot. He teaches in Paris at the *École des Beaux-Arts*, and in Saas-Fee, Switzerland, at the European Graduate School.

Barbara Beck is an American poet and translator currently living in Paris, France. Her poems have appeared in such journals as *Ekleksographia, Van Gogh's Ear, The Café Review*, and in the anthology *Strangers in Paris* (Tightrope Books, Toronto, 2011). New work is forthcoming in *women: poetry: migration (an anthology)* from Theenk Books (New York). Translations include poems by Vannina Maestri in *Aufgabe*; poems by Dominique Quélen in *Cerise Press* and *ParisLitUp*; and Cid Corman's collection *Livingdying* (translated in collaboration with Dominique Quélen), published in French as *Vivremourir* (L'Act Mem, 2008). Since 2002, she has been editor of *Upstairs at Duroc*, the English-language literary journal published in Paris.

Philippe Beck, born in 1963, is a poet, writer and philosopher. In 1994 Beck received his Doctor of Philosophy at l'Ecole des hautes études en sciences sociales in Paris under the direction of Jacques Derrida and has been Associate Professor HDR in Philosophy at the Centre Atlantique de Philosophie at the University of Nantes since 1995. Beck's first book of poetry, *Garde-manche hypocrite*, appeared in 1996. He has since published over 20 volumes of critically acclaimed poetry and prose including *Opéradiques* (Flammarion, 2014), awarded the Great Poetry Prize by the Académie française in 2015. In 2014 a scholarly volume devoted to his work, *Philippe Beck: un chant objectif aujourd'hui*, appeared with Corti Press, after the Colloque de Cerisy dedicated to his work in 2012.

Michael Bishop is a poet, translator, publisher and the author of numerous critical studies of modern and contemporary art and literature. Among his recent publications are *Contemporary French Art, 1 & 2*; *Dystopie et poïein, agnose et reconnaissance. Seize études sur la poésie française et francophone contemporaine* (2014); and, in the creative realm, *La Genèse maintenant, suivie de La Théorie de l'amour* (2011) and *Fluvial, Agnose et autres poèmes* (2014).

Béatrice Bonhomme, born in 1956, is a poet and lecturer at the University of Nice. With Hervé Bosio she founded the critical literary review *Nu(e)*, which has been publishing work by contemporary poets since 1994, and she has organised numerous poetry readings and research fora relating to poetry. She teaches on poetry and is in charge of the research strand Poièma at the University of Nice. Since writing her doctoral thesis on Pierre-Jean Jouve, she has published scholarly work on writers including Yves Bonnefoy, Philippe Jaccottet and Salah Stétié, and she runs the Society for the study of Pierre-Jean Jouve. She has published over thirty books of poetry and criticism.

Stéphane Bouquet is the author of six collections of poems including *Nos amériques* (2010) and *Les amours suivants* (2013), both with the publisher Champ Vallon, with a seventh following in autumn 2016. He has translated into French collections by the American poets Robert Creeley, Paul Blackburn, James Schuyler and Peter Gizzi. He is the screenwriter of 11 films, frequently collaborating with Sébastien Lifshitz. In *La Traversée* (The Crossing), an autobiographical film, he played himself. Though not a dancer at all, he collaborated with Mathilde Monnier on *Déroutes* and *frère&sœur*.

Macgregor Card is a poet and bibliographer living in Brooklyn. He was co-editor of *The Germ*. He is co-editing an anthology of the New York School. Recent poems have appeared in *The Brooklyn Rail*, *Aufgabe*, *The Recluse*, *KGB Lit*, *Fence* and *Best American Poetry*.

Anne-James Chaton, born in 1970, has published several books with Al Dante and joined the German record label Raster-Noton in 2011. He has given many performances in France and abroad. He has released albums with the Dutch post-rock band The Ex, with the English guitarist Andy Moor, and with the German musician Alva Noto. In 2013 he began a collaboration with singer and composer Nosfell, performer Phia Menard and choreographer François Chaignaud around the Icons project and the same year formed the trio HERETICS with Andy Moor and Thurston Moore, guitarist and singer from American band Sonic Youth. In 2016, he published his first novel with Gallimard. His visual works, drawn from his writing materials, have been the subject of several solo and group exhibitions in France and abroad.

Joshua Clover is a Professor of English Literature and Comparative Literature at University of California, Davis, and has visited at Cornell University; University of California, Berkeley; and University of Paris. He is the author of three books of poetry and three of cultural history and theory. His publications include *Red Epic* (Commune Editions, 2015) and *Riot.Strike.Riot: The New Era of Uprisings* (Verso, 2016). A winner of the Walt Whitman Award from the Academy of American Poets, he has appeared multiple times in *Best American Poetry* and *Best American Music Writing*; scholarly and poetic work has been translated into ten languages. He is a founding editor of Commune Editions.

Jean-Michel Espitallier, born in 1957, has published over twenty books and is among those poets who have redefined poetry in the contemporary period. He represents a generation of writers who adopt a variety of practices that bring them close to contemporary art, and is also himself a drummer. He operates in different and ever-changing modes, including instrumental rhythms, writing based on lists, logically absurd propositions and humour, and aims at inventing new forms to test the limits of language. He was the co-founder and co-director of the review *Java* (1989-2006), and he edited the dossier on 'New French Poetry' in the *Magazine littéraire* (2001).

Simone Fattal was born in Damascus and grew up in Lebanon. She studied philosophy at the École des Lettres of Beirut and then at the Sorbonne in Paris. In 1969 she returned to Beirut and started painting. She participated in numerous shows during the ten years when life in Lebanon was still possible. In 1980, fleeing the Civil War, she settled in California and founded the Post-Apollo Press, a publishing house dedicated to innovative and experimental literary work. In 1988, she returned to artistic practice by making ceramic sculptures after enrolling at the Art Institute of San Francisco. Since 2006, she has produced works in Hans Spinner's prestigious workshop in Grasse, France. In 2013, she released a movie, *Autoportrait*, which has been shown worldwide in many film festivals.

Simone Forti is a dancer, choreographer, artist and writer. In the spring of 1961 she presented a full evening of *Dance Constructions*, which proved to be influential in both the dance and the art world. Forti's continuing explorations, including studies of animal movements and of the dynamics of circling, have manifested as drawings and as holograms, as well as in performance including collaborations with musicians Charlemagne Palestine and Peter Van Riper. Forti's engagement with movement and language includes her *News* Animations, which are improvisations in movement and spoken word, as well as her books including *Handbook in Motion* (Nova Scotia College of Art and Design Press, 1974) and *Oh, Tongue*, published and edited by Fred Dewey for Beyond Baroque Literary Arts Center, 2003. Works of hers are included in the permanent collections of The Museum of Modern Art, New York; The Whitney Museum, New York; and The Stedelijk Museum, Amsterdam. In 2014 Forti had a retrospective show at the Museum der Modern in Salzburg, Austria. She received a Yoko Ono Lennon Award for Courage in the Arts in 2011 and is represented by The Box LA Gallery www.theboxla.com.

Jérôme Game is a French writer. Since 2000 he has published over fifteen books, various CDs of sound-poetry, a DVD of videopoems, and given many readings/performances in France and abroad (Europe, North Africa, Asia, America). His writing has developed through a series of collaborations with visual artists, musicians, stage directors and choreographers which explore points of contact between writing and other practices (images, on stage, sounds). Translation, correspondence, appropriation; re-initialization of processes, issues of cross-border, common *dispositifs*: it is within these gaps that his writing (re-)composes itself. In 2015 he had his first exhibition in Casablanca, Morocco. He has published in many reviews and his work has been translated into several languages (English, Spanish, Italian, Chinese, Japanese). He has also written theoretical texts on contemporary aesthetics. Latest publications include *Développements* (Manucius, 2015), *DQ/HK* (book+2CDs, L'Attente, 2013). Site: www.jeromegame.com

Jean-Marie Gleize, born in 1946, is a poet and academic. He has published over forty works of poetry and criticism, many of which with Le Seuil. His most recent work is *Le Livre des cabanes* published in Le Seuil's 'Fiction & Cie' collection in 2015. Since *Léman*, published in the same collection in 1990, he has pursued a meditation in prose ('prose in prose', 'post-poetry') which takes the form of an inquiry, a discontinuous narrative investigation (literal, documentary) starting from traces, physical data (photographs, polaroids, video) or texts. He is Emeritus Professor at l'École normale supérieure de Lyon where he directed the Centre d'études poétiques from 1999 to 2009. He edited the *NIOK* Collections (éditions Al Dante) and « Signes » (ENS éditions), and created the review *NIOQUES* which he has directed since 1990.

Abigail Lang is associate professor at Université Paris-Diderot, a translator of Anglophone poetry into French, a member of the Double Change collective (www.doublechange.org), and co-editor of the Motion Method Memory imprint at Les Presses du réel. Recent publications include a collection of essays on contemporary British poetry that she co-edited with David Nowell Smith (*Modernist Legacies. Trends and Faultlines in British Poetry Today,* Palgrave, 2015), the digital edition of the magazine *Change* (1968–1983) (Presses du réel, 2016) and translations, often made in collaboration: Rosmarie Waldrop, *La route est partout* (L'attente, 2011); Lorine Niedecker, *Louange du lieu* (Corti, 2013); John Ashbery and James Schuyler, *Un nid de nigauds* (Presses du réel,

2015); Lyn Hejinian, *Ma vie* (Presses du réel, 2016); Caroline Bergvall, *L'anglais medley* (Presses du réel, forthcoming).

Ellen LeBlond-Schrader is a poet and artist based in Paris and Detroit. Her poems and sound installations have been shown at Fondation Ricard (Paris), Museu Martins Sarmento (Portugal), Louis Vuitton Cultural Space (Paris), New Langton Arts (San Francisco), the Kadist Art Foundation (Paris), and Centre Pompidou (Paris). She is currently working on a project for Elevation 1049 in Gstaad, Switerland. She also translates poems, films and art criticism.

Kate Lermitte Campbell recently completed a DPhil at Oxford University. The title of her dissertation was *Thought, Perception and the Creative Act: A Study of the Work of Four Contemporary French Poets: Pierre Alferi, Valère Novarina, Anne Portugal and Christophe Tarkos*. She lives and works in London and Paris.

Sabine Macher was born in ten-year-old West Germany, a country that has vanished now. She left it for France in 1976, where she writes, translates, dances and takes small photographs that she looks at while traveling between Paris and elsewhere. She has published a dozen books, most recently *deux coussins pour Norbert* (éditions Le bleu du ciel, 2009) and *residence absolue* (éditions Isabelle Sauvage, 2011). *The l-notebook* (original title *carnet d'a*, LaPresse, 2014), translated by Eleni Sikelianos, is her first book in English.

Jean-Michel Maulpoix, born in 1952, is a scholar of modern and contemporary poetry and teaches at the Sorbonne Nouvelle. He is the author of volumes of poetry including *Une histoire de bleu*, *L'Écrivain imaginaire*, *Domaine public*, and *Pas sur la neige*, published with Mercure de France. He has also published critical works on Henri Michaux, Jacques Réda, René Char, Rainer Maria Rilke and Paul Celan, as well as essays on poetics, including *La poésie malgré tout*, *La poésie comme l'amour* and *Du lyrisme*. He considers that his writing, which combines poetry and prose, consists of 'critical lyricism'. He edits the digital literary review *Le Nouveau Recueil*.

Michèle Métail, born in 1950, studied German and Chinese and is the author of a doctorate on Chinese poetry. Since 1973 her poetry has been disseminated via public readings (of which she has given more than 500 in France and abroad). The projection of words in space represent the 'final stage of writing' for her, and her readings are often accompanied by slides and a recording. With the composer Louis Roquin she founded the Association Les arts contigus which examines connections and confrontations between the arts. She took part in Oulipo activities from time to time, but has not done so since 1998.

Sandra Moussempès, born in 1965 in Paris, is a poet. A former resident poet of the Villa Médicis of the Academy of France in Rome, she has contributed to various reviews and anthologies in France and abroad as well as publishing nine books mainly at Flammarion Publishing (including *Photogénie des ombres peintes*, *Acrobaties dessinées* and *Sunny girls*). She speaks of deciphering the mental codes that surround us through disrupting conventional imagery, in particular clichés about the feminine, through the creation of a troubling environment which often has cinematographic qualities or is inspired by sensations of déjà vu. She has translated Kristin Prevallet into French, and has been translated by Prevallet as well as Serge Gavronsky, Lee-Ann Brown and Carolyn Ducker. In the 1990s, she sang in several Paris- and London-based bands (she collaborated on The Wolfgang Press's final album, released by the British label 4AD). In keeping with her poetry, she is also a vocal and sound artist and has performed in various art museums and at poetry festivals.

Jennifer Moxley is the author of six books of poetry, most recently *The Open Secret* (2014), winner of the Poetry Society of America's William Carlos Williams award. She has also published a book of essays, *There are Things We Live Among*, and a memoir. In addition to her translation of Anne Portugal's *absolute bob*, she has translated two books by Jacqueline Risset, *Sleep's Powers* and *The Translation Begins*. Her poem 'Behind the Orbits' was included by Robert Creeley in *The Best American Poetry* 2002. She is Professor of Poetry and Poetics at the University of Maine. Site: jennifermoxley.com

Michelle Noteboom is the author of *Roadkill* (Corrupt Press, 2013), *The Chia Letters* (Dusie Kollektiv, 2009), *Edging* (Cracked Slab Books, 2006), which won the Heartland Poetry Prize, and *Hors-cage* (in French translation by Frédéric Forte, Editions de l'attente, 2010). Originally from Michigan, she has lived in Paris since 1991 where she translates films for the French audio-visual industry, and co-curated the Ivy Writers bilingual reading series with Jennifer K. Dick for over 10 years.

Gilles Ortlieb was born in 1953 in Ksar-Es-Souk, Morocco. He moved to France in the 1960s and studied Classics at the Sorbonne and then Modern Greek at the Institute of Oriental Languages in Paris. After a variety of jobs and travels in the Mediterranean region, he became a translator for the European Union in Luxemburg in 1986, and worked there for over twenty years. His first texts were published in the *Nouvelle Revue Française* in 1977, and he is the author of fifteen books, including prose, poetry, essays and notebooks. His most recent publications are *Tombeau des anges* (Gallimard, 2011), *Vraquier* (Finitude, 2013), and most recently, with Le Bruit du temps, 2016's *Et tout le tremblement* and a collection of literary essays entitled *Dans les marges.*

Anne Portugal is a poet and translator. She has published a dozen books, most of them with P.O.L, including *Les commodités d'une banquette* (1985); *De quoi faire un mur* (1987); *Le plus simple appareil* (1992), translated by Norma Cole as *Nude* with Kelsey St. Press; *définitif bob* (2001), translated by Jennifer Moxley as *absolute bob* with Burning Desk; *Voyez en l'air,* at éditions de l'Attente, translated by Rosmarie Waldrop as *quisite moment* with Burning Desk; and *la formule flirt* (2010), translated by Jean-Jacques Poucel as *the flirt formula* with la Presse. She translated, with Caroline Dubois, *Paramour* by Stacy Doris (P.O.L, 2010), and is now finishing, with Abigail Lang and Vincent Broqua, the translation of *Meddle english* by Caroline Bergvall, to be published by Presses du réel in 2016.

Christian Prigent, born in 1945, is the author of over forty works of poetry, fiction and criticism published mainly with P.O.L. He gives readings of his work regularly both in France and abroad. Provocative and ironic, he is a radical experimenter of form and his works attest to his battle with language. At the beginning of the 1970s, he co-founded the review *TXT* with Jean-Luc Steinmetz. An international conference dedicated to his work was held at the Cerisy-la-Salle Cultural Centre in July 2014.

Nathalie Quintane, born in 1964, published her first texts in poetry reviews. She subsequently published books with P.O.L (*Chaussure*, 1997; *Saint-Tropez*, 2001; *Tomates*, 2010; *Crâne chaud*, 2012) that were not classified by genre, as well as two novels. She has taken part in many public readings in France and abroad, and regularly works with artists. Her most recent publication is *Les années 10* (La Fabrique éditions, 2014).

Sarah Riggs is a writer and artist born in New York where she is now based, having spent over a decade in Paris. Before directing *Six Lives: A Cinepoem*, she produced *The Tangier 8* at the Cinémathèque de Tanger in Morocco, which was screened at the Berlin Film Festival and the Tate Modern Museum among other international venues. She is the author of five books of poetry in English: *Waterwork* (Chax, 2007), *Chain of Minuscule Decisions in the Form of a Feeling* (Reality Street, 2007), *60 Textos* (Ugly Duckling, 2010), *Autobiography of Envelopes* (Burning Deck, 2012), and *Pomme & Granite* (1913 Press, 2015) which won a 1913 poetry prize. She is the author of the book of essays *Word Sightings: Poetry and Visual Media in Stevens, Bishop, & O'Hara* (Routledge, 2002), and has translated and co-translated six books of contemporary French poetry into English. She is the director of the international arts organization Tamaas (www.tamaas.org) which has ongoing projects in performance, translation and artistic collaboration in Morocco and France. She is also a member of bilingual poetry association Double Change (www.doublechange.org).

Eléna Rivera is a poet and translator who was born in Mexico City and spent her formative years in Paris. She won the 2010 Robert Fagles prize for her translation of Bernard Noël's *The Rest of the Voyage* (Graywolf Press, 2011) and is a recipient of a 2010 National Endowment for the Arts Literature Fellowship in Translation. She has also translated three of Isabelle Baladine Howald's books, *Secret of Breath* (Burning Deck Press, 2009), *The Pain of Returning* (Mindmade Books, 2012) and *Parting Movement, Constantly Prevented* (Oystercatcher Press, 2014). Eléna's book of poems, *Scaffolding*, is forthcoming from Princeton University Press.

Stephen Romer is a poet, critic and translator. He has lived in France since 1981, where he teaches at the University François Rabelais at Tours. He has edited two major anthologies of modern French poetry: *Twentieth Century French Poems* (Faber, 2002) and, with Jennie Feldman, *Into the Deep Street: Seven Modern French Poets 1938–2008* (Anvil, 2009). Recent work in translation has included *The Arrière-pays* by Yves Bonnefoy (Seagull, 2012) and a collection of fin-de-siècle short stories *French Decadent Tales* (Oxford World Classics, 2013).

Bonnie Roy is a poet and scholar whose work has appeared in journals including *Contemporary Literature* and *Jubilat*. She teaches literature and writing at the University of California, Davis.

Keston Sutherland is the author of *The Odes to TL61P*, *The Stats on Infinity*, *Stress Position*, *Hot White Andy* and many other poems. His *Poetical Works 1999–2015* was published by Enitharmon in 2015. He lives in Brighton.

Cole Swensen, a writer born in San Francisco, has published fifteen volumes of poetry. Six of these have been translated into French by Maïtreyi and Nicolas Pesquès and published by José Corti, most recently *Si riche heure*, *L'Age de verre* and *Le nôtre*. Cole Swensen's own translations from French include texts by Suzanne Doppelt, Olivier Cadiot and Oscarine Bosquet. She received the PEN USA Award in Literary Translation in 2004.

Christophe Tarkos (1964–2004) was very active in poetry publishing, contributing to numerous reviews, from those produced on the smallest scale to the most prestigious, among them *Doc(k)s*, *TTC* and *Nioques*, and publishing volumes with various presses whether small or well known. He co-founded the reviews *RR* (with Stéphane Bérard and Nathalie Quintane, see above), *Quaderno* (with Philippe Beck, see above), *Poézi prolétèr* (with Katlin Molnar and Pascal Doury) and undertook various publishing activities with Charles Pennequin. He gave readings and performances at meetings and festivals, often in the company of Julien Blaine. His six publications with P.O.L are *Caisses* (1998), *Le Signe* (1999), *Pan* (2000), *Anachronisme* (2001) and the posthumous collections *Ecrits Poétiques* (2008) and *L'Enregistré* (2014). P.O.L are currently preparing his collected works.

Susan Wicks is a poet and fiction writer. Her translations of Valérie Rouzeau, *Cold Spring in Winter* and *Talking Vrouz* (Arc), have won the Scott Moncrieff and Oxford-Weidenfeld Prizes and been shortlisted for the Popescu Prize and the International Griffin Prize for Poetry. Her own seventh collection, *The Months* (Bloodaxe, 2016) is a Poetry Book Society Recommendation.